PREMIER LEAGUE
FOOTBALL

Italian Import Marco Branco lines up Middlesbrough's second against Liverpool.
Ross Kinnairdl/Allsport.

PREMIER LEAGUE
FOOTBALL

Michael Heatley

PARKGATE
BOOKS

PRC Publishing Ltd,
Kiln House, 210 New Kings Road, London SW6 4NZ

This edition published in 1998 by
Parkgate Books Ltd
Kiln House
210 New Kings Road
London SW6 4NZ
Great Britain

British Library Cataloguing in Publication Data:
A catalogue record for this book is available from the British Library.

ISBN 1 902616 146
Printed and bound in Italy

Contents

Introduction   6

League History   8

League Statistics   22

The Premiership Teams

Arsenal   28
Manchester Utd   36
Liverpool   44
Chelsea   52
Leeds United   60
Blackburn Rovers   68
Aston Villa   76
West Ham Utd   84
Derby County   92
Leicester City   100
Coventy City   108
Southampton   116
Newcastle United   124
Tottenham Hotspur   132
Wimbledon   140
Sheffield Wednesday   148
Everton   156

The Promoted Teams

Nottingham Forest   166
Middlesbrough   170
Charlton   174

The Relegated Teams

Bolton Wanderers   180
Barnsley   184
Crystal Palace   188

Introduction

The very first football in England may well have been played by the Romans, whose legions enjoyed an individual ball game that involved handling and physical contact. This was passed down to the public schools as rugby, the codes dividing in the 19th century and leaving us with what we now know as football, or soccer.

In the past decade, any number of rival pursuits—American (Gridiron) Football, personal computers, video recorders, satellite—have conspired to compete with the humble leather ball for the attention of youngsters destined to be stars of the future. Yet the game has survived and thrived because it has a century or more of history behind it. And at its highest level, the Premiership, English football has never been more media-friendly, with many of the world's leading names now competing every weekend.

The game's popularity has had a lot to do with its simplicity. It can be played almost anywhere by any number of players. And since its objective is simply to score more goals between two posts (rolled-up coats or what have you), its rules are easily understood. It was when the Football Association was set up in 1863 that those rules were officially codified, to be passed down to a waiting world. The Football League, set up 25 years later, proved a highly competitive example for others to follow. And the advent of the Premiership in 1992 has sent the game's profile through the roof.

As we stand on the threshold of a new millennium, following the euphoria of a world cup, the game the media once loved to hate, with its working-class connotations, hooligan image and blood and thunder tactics is certainly the sporting flavour of the month!

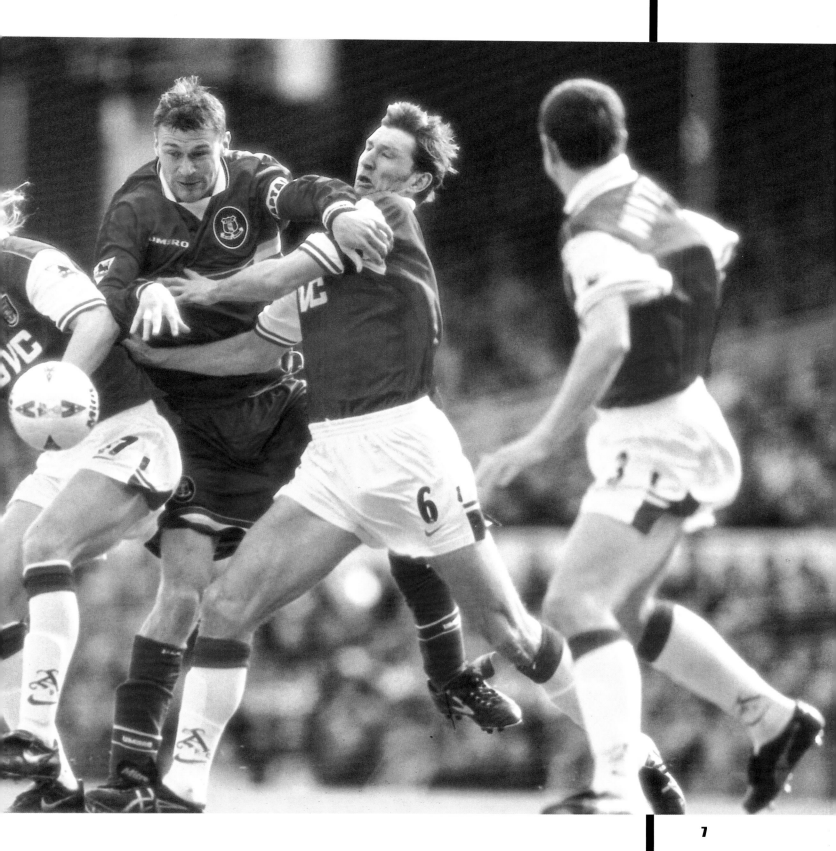

PREMIER LEAGUE FOOTBALL

Introduction

League History

No matter where you go in the world, English football is known and respected. Having originated the game as we know it today and founded the Football League, the model for countless other competitions throughout the world, in 1888, the English scene as represented by the Premiership of the late 1990s features superstars from all over the globe, having at last eclipsed Italy's Serie A as the most prestigious league in the world.

The formation of the Premiership in 1992 was an event which shook up the English game in the most radical way since the foundation of the Football League itself. The country's leading clubs broke away to establish their own Superleague under the auspices of the Football Association; funded by money from satellite television screening live matches, they were able to attract the biggest names in world football to the English game. More than this, they stemmed the 'talent drain' that saw names like Hoddle, Waddle, Gascoigne and Platt play their football in foreign countries where rewards were once greater.

The Football League remained in operation with the other 70 clubs excluded from the new elite—and while it could claim it had history on its side, its 'rival' had the resources to call all the shots. A 22-strong roster of Premiership clubs was reduced to 20 with the aim of reducing fixture congestion and there was talk about cutting the figure again to 18, though this controversial suggestion has yet to be implemented.

Many in the game, such as players' spokesman Gordon Taylor, initially disapproved of the Premiership: the PFA chef executive slammed the concept as 'a way for the leading clubs to seize virtually all the money, leaving the remaining clubs to wither and some to die'. Yet the plan went through regardless—and the marketing opportunities embraced by the Premiership, such as the revenue available from replica shirts, have now been echoed lower down the 'evolutionary chain'.

Clubs like Chelsea with their megastore selling everything from hats to Harley Davidson motorcycles had shown the way, underlining the fact that football in the 21st century was going to be much more than simply getting bums on seats. While Southampton looked to develop an out of town stadium to overcome their inability to extend their inner-city Dell, grounds like Manchester United's Old Trafford and Arsenal's Highbury were being developed to their utmost to meet a demand for their product that now clearly exceeded supply. The interest that greeted the World Cup was also proof that football consciousness had reached every level of society—although the all-too-familiar scenes in southern France produced television images that the squeaky-clean Premiership has not had to cope with following the Taylor report and more intensive policing.

The prospects for Premiership football have never looked so good, and England's early demise in the World Cup has only slightly dented the 'best league' image. The flood of World Cup stars to the Premiership, such as Desailly and Laudrup to Chelsea, means more of the colour and flair needed to keep the sport interesting.

Dare one say it, but the fact that Manchester United's impressive grip on the cup—four wins out of five Premiership years makes them easily the Premiership team of the 1990s— slipped to allow in a London club will also help to keep the championship fresh. Everyone likes a winner, but it is easy for a competition to get stale without some variety.

Arsenal certainly supplied that! Although London-based, the team had precious few Londoners in it. The main reason for this was the appointment in August 1996 of French coach Arsène Wenger, who had made his name with French champions Monaco before enjoying a spell in Japanese exile. His appointment in place of Bruce Rioch not only raised

eyebrows—he was hardly a household name—but presaged an influx of foreign talent at managerial level; north London neighbours Tottenham would follow suit a year later with Swiss national boss Christian Gross. The cultured, quietly spoken Frenchman had an enormous impact on the Highbury team's training, diet and style and sensibly did not dismantle the foundations laid by Rioch's predecessor, George Graham. The communication on the pitch belied the many languages of the players. After a slow start when many fans questioned Wenger's judgement and the wisdom of spending record sums on foreign imports while dispensing with the services of Gunners fans' favourite, Paul Merson, the team's post-Christmas run to the Championship displayed exhilarating football of the highest order. They played 17 games, winning 15 and drawing two, losing only after the cup had been presented to the team at Highbury after the Everton game.

The team was built on a rock-like English defence that let in less than a goal a game—33 in all—and led Wenger to question why Seaman, Winterburn, Adams, Bould, Keown and Dixon haven't played regularly for England. The midfield was built around two muscular yet gifted Frenchmen, Emmanuel Petit and Patrick Vieira, who proved to be the dynamo on which the title effort ran, and combative Englishman Ray Parlour, who was unlucky not to join the England team for France '98. Petit and Vieira did see action in the World Cup Final for France and combined together for Petit's brilliant goal against Brazil. In attack there was flair in abundance—Marc Overmars was brought in from Ajax to burst through from wide on the left to support fellow countryman Dennis Bergkamp, who scored the goal of the World Cup with a deft move he'd practised in the 1997-98 season in the Premiership game against Leicester. Forward options were multiplied by Liberian Christopher Wreh (a cousin of George Weah) and French teenager Nicolas Anelka. Their recruitment was fortunate given the injury-ravaged season endured by first-choice Ian Wright, Anelka notably blossoming when given an extended run.

In the end, Paul Merson was not missed as Arsenal steadily overhauled Manchester United from the turn of the year. It was not unlike their stealthy eclipse of Liverpool in 1989, except that this time the FA Cup would be the icing on the cake. A 2-0 defeat of

PREMIER LEAGUE FOOTBALL

League History

Newcastle gave Arsenal the Double for the second time ever, equalling the triumph of Bertie Mee's team in 1971. Fittingly, Pat Rice, the stalwart right-back of that side, was Wenger's assistant.

It was all a long way from 26 October 1863, when eleven clubs sent representatives to the Freemasons Tavern in central London to form 'a football association . . . for the purpose of settling a code of rules for the regulation of the game.' The first annual general meeting took place in the last week in September, thus setting the beginning of the traditional football season.

In echoes of the Premiership, not all those present gave their backing to the new Football Association. Charterhouse, one of the 'great schools', agreed with the broad aims of the association but captain BF Hartshorne felt he had to wait to gauge the reaction of others before giving up their own brand of the game. Harrow, too, were initially unwilling to change their rules—but when the FA rules were finally agreed upon in early December, they were based on that school's understanding of how the game was played.

By that time, Rugby had resigned from the new association, not because they liked to handle the ball but because the practice of 'hacking' or physically kicking opponents was outlawed. The Rugby Football Union was formed in 1871 by those for whom handling and hacking held no fears.

Rules agreed by the FA included the maximum length and breadth of the pitch, kicking off, goals, throw-ins and offside. Corners were free-kicks taken 15 yards from the goal line opposite where the ball went out of play. Passing the ball by hand was still permitted if caught 'fairly or on the first bounce.' Yet the rules were strangely non-specific in such matters as number of players, the penalty for foul play or even the shape of the ball, such matters to be decided by agreement between the captains.

Incomplete as these basic rules were, they were a start—and competition was soon to follow. The first New Year fixture between Sheffield and Nottingham was played on 2 January 1865: the latter (now Notts County) are thus the oldest current League club, having been founded two years earlier. Sheffield ventured to London in the following year, but having won the first Nottingham fixture found themselves losing to the capital outfit.

Nottingham Forest were formed In 1865, and the first 'derby' game against local rivals County followed. Chesterfield (1866) and Stoke (1867) were next to join, and the game spread, no longer the exclusive preserve of the public schools but not yet a working-class pastime.

Sheffield's game in London in 1866 had enabled the FA to observe their rules at close quarters, and handling and catching the ball was soon abolished as a result. The FA Cup was clearly the start of something big. Within a matter of a few years, all clubs vied to take part—and by doing so accepted the FA rules of football which remain the basis by which the game is played throughout the world today.

If the FA kicked off organised football in England, then the foundation of the Football League in 1888 gave it a huge kick forward. Ironically, its founder was a Scotsman—William McGregor, a man who never played a game of first-class football in his life. He organised the two meetings held in London and Manchester which brought together the 12 clubs soon to become the League's founder members: Accrington, Aston Villa, Blackburn Rovers, Bolton Wanderers, Burnley, Derby County, Everton, Notts County, Preston North End, Stoke, West Bromwich Albion and Wolverhampton Wanderers.

With the FA Cup the only current competition, clubs' revenue depended on a good run: an early exit could be disastrous, while friendly games postponed due to Cup replays were often not replayed. The League was formed to create order from chaos, give a structure to the game in England and guarantee fixtures and revenue for the country's top dozen teams. These were split equally between the north and the midlands, the south remaining predominantly amateur.

Preston North End achieved the League and Cup Double in the first season, finishing the season undefeated and without having conceded a Cup goal. The team was mainly made up of Scots, England centre forward John Goodall the star 'foreigner'.

Preston also won the League the following year, despite four defeats, with runners-up Everton reversing positions in the 1890-91 season. The 12 founder members become 14 in 1891-92 with the addition of Stoke and Darwen.

Football League points were originally earned only for wins, but this was amended after ten weeks of the first season to award one point for the draw. That's how it stayed until 1981-82 when a large number of goalless draws led the League to up the points for a win to three.

Added to the League in 1890 when Stoke dropped out, Sunderland dominated the 1890s with three League titles in four seasons, their success setting up the north-east as a hotbed of football. Known as the Team of All the Talents, they topped 100 goals for the first time in League history in 1892-93, their first Championship season, due to the expansion of the division to 16 clubs.

Aston Villa were the first club to challenge northern supremacy, taking the title in 1893-94 and adding four more before the end of the century. A monopoly was avoided by Sheffield United, winners in 1897-98, who'd joined the League in 1893, a year after city rivals Wednesday.

The Football League acquired a 12-strong Second Division in 1892-93 by taking over the rival Football Alliance set up in 1889. The new division admitted its first club from the south in 1893 when Woolwich Arsenal were elected.

Promotion and relegation was settled by a series of three test matches, the top three teams from the Second Division playing the bottom three from the First. The system was simplified after a goalless draw in 1898 between Stoke and Burnley which kept both clubs in the top flight. An automatic two up/two down system of promotion and relegation was instituted that would remain until 1973-74, the third place being made the subject of a play-off in 1986-87.

The first years of the 20th Century up to World War I saw attendances booming—and Newcastle were a dominant force. Only a Cup Final defeat against Villa dashed their hopes

Below: *Nick Barnby attempts a dramatic clearance in Everton's 0–2 defeat by Spurs on 20 November 1997.*
Shaun Botterill/Allsport

PREMIER LEAGUE FOOTBALL

League History

of the Double, while 1907 and 1909 brought further Championship wins. In 1910 they finally won the Cup and, with five Final appearances, could consider themselves unlucky not to have done the Double. Their playmaker was Scots half-back Peter McWilliam, while a defence marshalled by Alec Gardner and Andy Aitken conceded just 33—less than a goal a game—in their 1904-05 League win. Apart from a double title win by Sheffield Wednesday in 1902-03 and 1903-04, the Championship changed hands with regularity. Lancashire staked a claim in the shape of Blackburn, whose prewar team won two Championships in 1912 and 1914 led by skipper Bob Crompton.

The First Division was extended by two clubs after the First World War, southern sides Arsenal and Chelsea taking the new places. But the north continued to dominate in the shape of Huddersfield whose hat-trick of titles in 1923-26 was masterminded by the great Herbert Chapman. Ironically, Arsenal would break the stranglehold after his move south.

Everton's 102 goals brought them the title in 1927-28 thanks to the great Bill 'Dixie' Dean, who beat George Camsell's 59-goal record (established just the previous year when Middlesbrough achieved promotion to the First Division) by a single strike.

The lower echelons of the League were expanded by a Third Division of 22 clubs, established in 1920-21. But after just one campaign the decision was made to regionalise the lower orders, with two Third Divisions serving the north (20 clubs) and south (22). By 1923-24 all four divisions numbered 22 clubs apiece, while 1950-51 would see the lower divisions expand yet again by adding an extra two clubs each.

The regional divisions fed one club apiece to the Second Division, teams in the Midlands, such as Mansfield Town and Walsall, being obliged to switch depending on the location of promotion and relegation candidates. In 1957-58 regionalisation was abandoned and the bottom halves of both tables amalgamated as the new Fourth Division.

Back in the top flight, Arsenal were carrying all before them thanks to manager Herbert Chapman, ironically a former player with north London rivals Spurs. Having set Huddersfield on the way to their third consecutive title, he succeeded Leslie Knighton at Highbury just as the offside law changed in the attackers' favour. Chapman withdrew the

centre-half from midfield to plug the gap in front of the goalkeeper, changing the course of football tactics as he did so.

Arsenal's success was founded on teamwork, talented individuals such as Buchan, James, Bastin and centre-half Herbie Roberts the foundations. But reputation was no guarantee of a place: the Cup-winning side of 1930 contained only four players who had lost 1-0 to Cardiff just three years before. The trophy came to the capital for the first time ever in 1931, and again in 1933—a year ironically remembered for their FA Cup Third Round giant-killing by Walsall. Chapman's death in 1934 didn't halt Arsenal's progress: they won the League twice more in 1933-34 and 1934-35 under George Allison, a Cup win in 1936 and a fifth Championship in 1937-38 confirming them as the team of the 1930s.

The war years saw football continue in Britain on a regional basis, but there was no substitute for League fare. As the hostilities ended and the English League programme restarted, the British public returned in their thousands. The 1948-49 season saw crowds at record levels, an aggregate figure of 41,271,424 that has never been surpassed—and with new all-seater stadia never will.

Liverpool won the first postwar First Division title, taking over from Merseyside neighbours Everton, Champions of 1938-39 who'd reigned through the war years. Arsenal, winners in 1948, gave way to Portsmouth whose Championships in 1949 and 1950 remain their only honours to date.

The 1950s saw English football wake up to advances elsewhere in the world. While Wolves, three times League Champions in 1954, 1958 and 1959, were undoubtedly a great team, their 3-2 defeat of Hungary's Honved in December 1954 could not justify newspaper headlines of 'World Champions' after the Hungarian national team had humbled England at Wembley in November 1953 and again six months later.

Above: *Former Liverpool Manager Kenny Dalglish continued the success laid by his predesesors Bill Shankley, Bob Paisley and Joe Fagan by winning the double in his first managerial season. He is the only manager along with the Brian Clough to win the championship with two different clubs.*
Stu Forster/Allsport

Nevertheless Wolves, fashioned by player turned manager Stan Cullis and captained by England's Billy Wright, were a class side. Wing-halves Eddie Clamp and Ron Flowers were the engine room, with keeper Bert Williams an ever-reliable last line of defence. Wolves' long-ball game was aimed at the head of striker Roy Swinbourne. But Manchester United, who finished top of the table in 1956 and 1957, were the team of the moment. Known as the Busby Babes, their talent was to flower briefly and brightly before the Munich air crash in February 1958. United's Duncan Edwards became the youngest postwar player to wear a full England shirt when he was capped at the age of 18 years and 6 months against Scotland in April 1955. (The record would endure until 1998, when it would be beaten by Liverpool's Michael Owen.)

The traditional Lancashire powerbase would be weakened by the advent of freedom of contract and the lifting of the maximum wage, two forces that would combine to make it impossible for such clubs to hold onto their stars. Blackpool, Burnley and Preston all enjoyed their last tastes of First Division power in this period: Blackpool finished runners-up to Manchester United in 1956, Preston to Wolves two years later while Burnley's Championship in 1959-60 was only their second in 72 years!

The maximum wage was abolished in 1961 after George Eastham challenged Newcastle United's right to refuse him a transfer in a court of law. The 'retain and transfer' system had previously existed unchallenged, and now a player had the right to decide his own destiny (thanks to Jimmy Hill, now a TV pundit but then chairman of the Professional Footballers' Association) it was time for market forces to rule.

At the bottom end of the scale, the abolition of regional football in 1958 had increased the cost of running a team, and it was surprising that only one club, Accrington Stanley in 1961-62, went out of business. Elsewhere, Fulham hung onto their England midfielder Johnny Haynes by making him the first £100 a week footballer, while Denis Law and Jimmy Greaves returned from Italian exile to join Manchester United and Spurs—two clubs whose buying power would help them become established as 1960s giants.

Spurs' Double triumph of 1960-61 came the season before Greaves' arrival and, settling old scores, equalled neighbours' Arsenal's record points total set in 1930-31. It was masterminded by two managers—Bill Nicholson, the official Tottenham chief, and midfield man Danny Blanchflower, who proved an inspirational captain. 'In a poor side, Danny was a luxury,' said Nicholson, 'but in a good side his creativity was priceless.'

Blanchflower was an Irishman, and indeed only full-back Peter Baker and Ron Henry were locally-born, a fact that illustrated the changing nature of football. Another influential 'foreigner' was Dave Mackay, not long arrived from Hearts in Scotland, who would pick up a Second Division Championship medal in 1969 with Derby in the twilight of his career. This, plus the Footballer of the Year accolade, would prove some recompense for two broken legs that blighted his time at Spurs.

Denis Law's arrival at Old Trafford was the signal for Manchester United to resume the run of success that had ended at Munich: Matt Busby's record of five Championship wins in 15 years—1952, 1956, 1957, 1965 and 1967—shows the eight-year gap it took him to rebuild. Irish international goalkeeper Harry Gregg, centre-half Bill Foulkes and Bobby Charlton were three Munich survivors who were to play their part in the later glory.

Charlton, who emerged from the north-east with his brother Jack (who signed for Leeds), scored twice on his United debut at 19. Initially a centre-forward, he found greatest success as a deep-lying left-winger with a powerful shot.

As well as Scotsman Law, Belfast winger George Best would feed on the midfield skills of Pat Crerand and ball-winner Nobby Stiles to create footballing magic. The peak undoubtedly came in 1967 and 1968 with first the League Championship and then a European Cup win against Benfica at Wembley. But such achievement could not be sustained indefinitely, and only in the 1990s under Alex Ferguson would United regain their crown as kings of the English game.

Back in the 1960s, football in the north-west was far from a one-city story. The arrival of certain William Shankly at Anfield in December 1959 started a Merseyside revolution. Promotion to the top flight followed in 1961-62 and ushered in an era of success that continued under his successors Bob Paisley, Joe Fagan and Kenny Dalglish until the early 1990s.

Across Stanley Park at Everton, former favourite Harry Catterick arrived from Sheffield Wednesday to replace Johnny Carey, who'd brought players like Vernon, Young and Gabriel to Merseyside without finding success. Catterick built on this to take the Championship in 1962-63, and with Liverpool winning the title three years later a 'leapfrog' effect was set up that would quickly establish Merseyside alongside Manchester as the premier football city. Liverpool's Roger Hunt and Goodison star Ray Wilson both played key roles in England's World Cup victory in 1966, and were joined on Merseyside by Alan Ball of Blackpool who arrived at Goodison later that summer. Emlyn Hughes followed the route but to Liverpool and like Ball would captain England in the 1970s as well as lead Liverpool to domestic and European success.

Everton's cultured brand of football led to Goodison being dubbed the School of Science. Catterick had built his team around the midfield trio of Howard Kendall, Ball and Colin Harvey, while his Anfield counterpart had used a central backbone of three Scots—keeper Tommy Lawrence, centre-half Ron Yeats and centre-forward Ian St John. The two approaches were as different as were the managers' own characters.

A new generation of Liverpool stars came to the fore under Bob Paisley, who succeeded Shankly in 1974. Three years later he replaced Kevin Keegan with Kenny Dalglish, and teamed him with another Scot and future manager in Graeme Souness. Six League Championships came under Paisley, the 1979 trophy lifted with just 16 goals conceded thanks to Alan Hansen marshalling the defence. Ian Rush scored 17 goals in his first full season, 1981-82, to help achieve another title, while 1981 saw the European Cup raised for the third time after Real Madrid were beaten 1-0 in Paris. A hat-trick of consecutive League Cup wins preceded Paisley's retirement in 1983.

While nowhere near as consistent as neighbours United, Manchester City were one of the most attractive teams to watch in the late 1960s and early 1970s. Under Joe Mercer's stewardship, they won all three domestic trophies—League, FA and League Cup—in successive seasons, while the Second Division title and European Cup Winners' Cup came within a concurrent six-year spell. Mercer and assistant 'Big Mal' Allison nurtured such talents as England internationals Francis Lee, Mike Summerbee, Colin Bell and Rodney Marsh, while veteran defender Tony Book, a bargain buy from Allison's old club Plymouth, went on to manage the club in later years.

Aside from Liverpool, the biggest challenge to Manchester superiority came from Leeds United whose uncompromising football was cast in the image of manager Don Revie. He joined Leeds from Sunderland in 1958, becoming player-manager three years later.

Promotion to the top flight in 1964 preceded two League titles (in 1969 and 1974) and the FA Cup in 1972—but three losing Finals and five second places in the League made them the nearly men of English football. European success came with the Fairs (now UEFA) Cup in 1968 and 1971, but Revie's decision to take the England manager's job in 1974 led to the disastrous (and very brief) reign of Brian Clough and a decline from the high standards Revie had demanded until Howard Wilkinson, another disciplinarian, took Leeds back to the top in the 1990s.

Leeds' team of the 1970s was made up almost entirely of internationals, from Scot David Harvey who replaced Welsh cap Gary Sprake in goal to the international forward line of Lorimer (Scotland), Giles (Eire), Clarke (England) and Gray (Scotland). While much retrospective criticism has been made of their 'take no prisoners' attitude, at their best (as in a 7-0 demolition of Southampton in March 1972) they did not disgrace the all-white strip Revie modelled on all-conquering Real Madrid.

With fellow north Londoners Tottenham the last team to achieve the coveted League and Cup Double, Arsenal's repeat achievement ten years later in 1970-71 must have tasted 'doubly' sweet. The man who masterminded their success was ex-physio Bertie Mee, in his first managerial job, but there were plenty of footballing brains on the pitch in the likes of captain Frank McLintock and George Graham. Both became managers in their turn, Graham enjoying several seasons of success at Highbury in the 1990s.

If the Gunners were the team of the early 1970s, the manager of the decade had to be Brian Clough. He won the Championship with two different and wildly unfashionable clubs—Derby in 1972 and Nottingham Forest in 1978—as well as securing two back-to-back League Cup wins and, his greatest achievement, successive European Cups in 1979 and 1980. Whether solo, as in later years, or in combination with assistant Peter Taylor, he

PREMIER LEAGUE FOOTBALL

League History

Above: *Ryan Giggs seen here in a Premiership clash against Liverpool was one of the original Ferguson fledgings. He has been instrumental in Manchester United's dominance in the 1990s.* Ben Radford/Allsport

Below: *Dutchman Dennis Bergkamp, signed by previous manager Bruce Rioch, spearheaded Arsenal's relentless charge for the League and Cup double.* Alex Livesey/Allsport

proved a motivator without equal, even if his unique and individual style tended to rub certain board members up the wrong way.

It was undoubtedly this abrasive streak to his character that ruled Clough out of a crack at the England job which surely should have been his. He'd only won two caps as a centre-forward for Sunderland in the late 1950s before injury curtailed his career (son Nigel would follow in his footsteps), but turned to management—initially with Hartlepool in 1965—with even greater success. 'He could be an absolute bastard,' said one of the players he boosted to international status, 'but you'd give him your last penny.'

Derby, under his inspirational leadership, rose from Second Division mediocrity to League Champions, Clough's rescuing of Dave Mackay from the soccer scrapheap a major factor. Roy McFarland, Alan Hinton and John O'Hare were bargain buys—£75,000 the three—and augmented by the likes of international defenders Todd and Nish took the title to the Baseball Ground for the first time.

An acrimonious departure was followed by short stints at Brighton and Leeds, neither successful. But 1975 saw him alight on yet another club with potential, Nottingham Forest, and he brought them hitherto undreamed-of honours. After taking the League for very first time in 1978, the 1979 European Cup was secured by a goal from Trevor Francis, Britain's first million-pound player (now Birmingham City manager), who also featured in a League Cup win against Southampton that brought a second trophy to the City Ground sideboard. Incredibly the European Cup was retained the following year, and Forest were rarely out of the Top 10 during the 1980s. Sadly, Clough's reign at Forest ended with relegation from the Premier League in 1993, but this did not diminish his achievements.

Forest were, along with Liverpool, the last English club to dominate Europe. The events in the Heysel Stadium, Brussels, in 1985 when Liverpool faced Juventus in the European Cup Final led to a ban on English clubs entering European competition—and though this was rescinded in 1990, success proved hard to come by thereafter as clubs and individuals strove to re-acclimatise themselves to the European way of playing.

Ironically, the first club to suffer was Liverpool's rivals Everton, Champions in 1985 under player turned manager Howard Kendall. They won again in 1987, despite the loss of star forward Gary Lineker who'd moved to Barcelona after his successful 1986 World Cup. Arsenal were the only other club to interrupt Liverpool's run of Championships in the late 1980s, cruelly killing the Reds' Double dream with a 2-0 win at Anfield in the last League game of the 1988-89 season. Goalscorer Michael Thomas must have impressed, since he became a Liverpool player two years later. He has recently moved to Benfica.

Arsenal would win the title again in 1991 despite having two points deducted for disciplinary reasons following an on-pitch brawl with Manchester United (who lost one point). Their manager George Graham added flair to a team built on the defensive rock of

centre-backs Tony Adams and David O'Leary by buying Swedish international winger Anders Limpar—but it was when allegations of financial inducements were made concerning the signing of other Scandinavian stars that he lost his job.

For a spell, Graham had locked horns with former Chelsea team-mate Terry Venables, who returned to English football after a glorious couple of seasons with Barcelona to take the top job at Tottenham. It was he who united the mercurial talents of Paul 'Gazza' Gascoigne and star England striker Gary Lineker to fashion a team that continued Spurs' tradition of winning Cups in years that ended with 1, but also restored their reputation as one of the League's 'flair' teams. It was his success with a predominantly English-born squad that impressed the FA when they looked for a national manger to replace Graham Taylor in 1994. By that time, the nature of the English scene which Venables had come home to take part in had changed.

This revolution had resulted from the foundation of the FA Premier League in 1992, an event which shook up the English game in the most radical way since 1888. When the larger clubs broke away from Football League control the FA accepted them with open arms, conferring respectability on a tactic that effectively divided the 92 League clubs for the first time into the haves and the have nots.

The new operation soon gained sponsorship from brewers Carling, and even more importantly tapped into Rupert Murdoch's Sky satellite TV channel. While highlights were still to be shown on BBC's Match Of The Day, certain games were moved to Sunday and Monday for live transmission on satellite—a move which both annoyed the traditionalists and cemented Sky's position as the UK's dominant non-terrestrial TV channel.

Longer-term effects of the move were soon to be seen. Top-level clubs dropping into the Endsleigh League (as the sponsored Football League now styled itself) were given a compensation package, but often found themselves paying Premier League wages for players pulling four-figure crowds. The need to bounce back straight away was vital, or lack of resources would lead to a permanent loss of status.

Another double-edged revolution to hit British football in the 1990s came with the widespread import of foreign players. While Tottenham's move to bring in Argentine World Cup heroes Ardiles and Villa in 1978 had met with unqualified success, precious few 'imports' stayed the course: Dutchmen Muhren and Thijssen at Ipswich were two other worthwhile 1970s arrivals.

With the European Community sweeping aside barriers and the collapse of the Iron Curtain allowing their players unprecedented freedom of movement, English football was inundated by a tidal wave of foreign players. Some, like France's Eric Cantona and Germany's Jürgen Klinsmann, were undoubtedly world class, but others were no better than the home-grown article. And, with foreign players available at 'duty-free' prices, the trickle-down effect of transfer fees to lower-division clubs was being hit badly.

Managers in the 1990s had the whole world to choose from—and did. But there could still only be so many winners and one of them was Scots boss Alex Ferguson. Having taken Aberdeen to European glory in 1983 and enjoyed a spell as national manager in succession to Jock Stein, he moved south of the border to take the hottest seat in English club football—and overcame the odds to become the first Manchester United supremo to emerge completely and utterly from the long shadow cast by Matt Busby.

His team that won the Premier League twice in its first two seasons featured a blend of shrewd domestic buys—like midfielders Roy Keane and Paul Ince—alongside comparative veterans like Steve Bruce and England dynamo Bryan Robson. A pair of imported international stars, Danish keeper Peter Schmeichel and volatile French forward Eric Cantona, topped off the package.

Yet with United's image and popularity having rebounded to 1960s levels and beyond, a large number of promising young players were gravitating to Old Trafford. The first of these soon emerged to join Ryan Giggs in the team, most notably David Beckham, Nicky

Above: *Blackburn keeper Tim Flowers holds aloft the Trophy in 1995 having won the Premiership by a single point after losing away to Liverpool 2-0, while Manchester United could only muster a draw at West Ham.*
Shaun Botterill/Allsport

League History

Above: *Stan Collymore's transfers in England have amounted to more £18 million. He is seen here shielding the ball from Adrian Matei of Bucharest, in a UEFA Cup tie.* Allsport

Butt and Gary Neville, who had become an England regular after what seemed a handful of games in a red shirt. His brother Phil also won a place alongside the high-priced stars.

United's first win had ended 26 years of frustration since the title had last been collected under the great Sir Matt Busby. Seven successive wins to end the campaign ensured closest challengers Aston Villa were seen off, former Old Trafford manager Ron Atkinson denied the spice of a victory over the club that sacked him in 1986. That season, 1992-93, also saw Brian Clough end his participation in football by resigning as manager of Nottingham Forest, who were relegated. He had sealed his own fate by not adequately replacing England striker Teddy Sheringham. Another departure of a more permanent variety in February was former national captain Bobby Moore, a victim of cancer.

In contrast to the United-Villa rivalry of the first Premiership season, 1993-94 was a cakewalk for United. Only once all season did their name fail to top the pile, and that was after the third match of the season when a draw with Newcastle placed them third. They also achieved the Double with a 4-0 Cup Final thrashing of Chelsea, ironically the only team to have beaten them twice in the Premiership. Just two more defeats came in a season that had featured a 22-match unbeaten run and confirmed their superiority. Pre-eminent was Eric Cantona, signed from Leeds the previous term, who top-scored for the club and hit two goals, both penalties, in the FA Cup Final. Though United flopped abroad, going out of the European Cup to Turks Galatasaray, Arsenal beat Parma against the odds in Copenhagen to take the European Cup Winners Cup.

London clubs were not going to take Old Trafford's domination lying down. Jürgen Klinsmann, Germany's legendary striker, spent the 1994-95 season at White Hart Lane, forming a multi-national strikeforce with England's sharpshooting Teddy Sheringham, while Spurs' rivals Arsenal swooped to secure the services of Dutchman Dennis Bergkamp in 1995 as Klinsmann returned to Munich. Every Premier club, it seemed, had at least one overseas star on their books.

If the fans were now enjoying more cosmopolitan fare, then the Taylor Report, which came into effect in August 1994, changed the way they watched the game. It had been inspired by a tragedy that took place at Hillsborough in 1989 during an FA Cup semi-final between Liverpool and Nottingham Forest. Crowds penned in by the anti pitch-invasion fences were crushed by those coming into the Leppings Lane end, and 96 Liverpool fans died in the most devastating tragedy ever to hit the game in England. It was 43 years since a comparable crowd incident at Bolton, when gatecrashers climbed over turnstiles to swell an already packed Burnden Park, but just four years after a fire at Bradford City's Valley Parade during a game had cost 56 lives and inspired the Popplewell Report.

Taylor went further, turning the spotlight on the dilapidated nature of many grounds, the matchday procedures with which spectators were policed and the balance that had to be struck between anti-hooligan measures and spectator safety. It was resolved as a result of this that all-seater stadia should be in place for the 1994-95 season for the top two divisions, subject to some unavoidable exceptions. The lower two divisions would be allowed to have standing fans until 1999.

The result was an overhaul not only of stadia but of attitudes towards football fans. No longer would they be treated as caged animals, it was reasoned, but facilities would be provided to make football the family game—a rethink that had come rather late in the day given the large number of diversions now available for youngsters who, even a decade ago, would have regarded kicking a ball in the street and watching their favourite team on a Saturday as natural pastimes.

Outfits like Aldershot and Maidstone had already been forced to quit the League within the past decade as dwindling crowds at the lower end of the League spectrum failed to pay higher wages. The argument grew that the return of regionalisation and/or part-time football was the only way to ensure the survival of teams outside the elite, but it was those at the gateway of the promised land who were first to make waves. A meeting of chairmen of the League's First Division clubs in late 1995 rejected a plan to declare independence and leave the Football League, opting instead for a compromise offer of a bigger share of the League's financial cake from TV and sponsorship deals. It was clear, however, that the potential was there for further splits in the ranks. It was up to the League to take a visionary stance and ring-fence its assets lest a Premier Division Two reduce it to an unviable rump.

Meanwhile, the European Court's ruling in 1995's Jean-Marc Bosman case meant that players at the end of their contracts could cross national borders without fees. The result was that many big names could, at the end of their contracts, choose to play in England in a reverse of the talent drain that had seen so many home-grown giants—Jimmy Greaves, Denis Law and John Charles, to name but three—pass in the opposite direction decades earlier. The return of England captain David Platt from four-season exile in Serie A was further proof that the Premier League could regard itself as among the world's most prestigious competitions—a fact reinforced by the late 1995 arrival of Brazilian superstars Juninho and Branco on Wearside to play for Middlesbrough.

Boro's new Riverside Stadium typified the purpose-built out of town venues that more and more clubs were considering offered the best way forward in providing 21st Century-standard entertainment for their public. North-east rivals Sunderland would move, too—in their case from historic Roker Park to the purpose-built Stadium of Light in nearby Wearmouth.

The Premiership trophy had a new name on it in 1995, Blackburn Rovers denying Manchester United a hat-trick of wins. Rovers owed much to £3.6 million striker Alan Shearer, but the man in charge whose tactics proved decisive was Kenny Dalglish, who had already proved his managerial mettle at Liverpool before his shock resignation in 1991. Millionaire chairman Jack Walker was the man who bankrolled Dalglish's dreams, and the side he created included not only England Number 9 Shearer but also fellow national team-mates Tim Flowers (goalkeeper), Graeme Le Saux (defender) and David Batty (midfielder).

A tremendous international prospect, striker Chris Sutton signed from Norwich for £5 million, shared the scoring duties up front, but would write himself out of England contention in 1998 when declining to play in the B team. Goals from the so-called SAS part-

Above: *Chelsea's and England's Graham Le Saux— seen in possession during the Premiership clash with Spurs on 12 April 1998 which Chelsea won 2–0—has been one of the major successes of the Chelsea revolution at Stamford Bridge.*
Mark Thompson/Allsport

Left: *Dan Petrescu and Dennis Wise close in on Frenchman David Ginola during Chelsea's 2–0 defeat of Spurs at Stamford Bridge on 12 April 1998.*
Mark Thompson/Allsport

League History

Right: *Michael Owen, seen in a Liverpool pre-season friendly against Linfield, has been a sensation for Liverpool and for England in the World Cup.* Allsport

nership secured the honours, Shearer 34 (10 penalties) and Sutton 15, with Scottish international Colin Hendry dominant in defence. Though Manchester United beat Blackburn home and away, they compounded the disappointment of finishing second with FA Cup Final defeat to Everton by a single goal. The Red Devils also bowed out of the European Cup early, and while they were boosted by the arrival of Andy Cole in mid season they lost Eric Cantona two matches later. He was banned and barely escaped jail following his infamous kung-fu kick at a Selhurst Park spectator in January 1995, missing the rest of the season as a consequence.

Blackburn's only previous Championship wins had come in 1911-12 and 1913-14—and if that put them firmly into the sleeping giant category, then Newcastle United, next season's pace-setters, had been little better. Last crowned as English Champions in 1927, they had endured decades of underachievement, briefly lit up by a hat-trick of FA Cup wins in the 1950s and a European trophy in 1969. The catalyst for their emergence as a real force was Kevin Keegan, whose arrival as a player alongside Paul Gascoigne and Chris Waddle had propelled the Magpies back to the top flight in 1984.

Keegan had returned as manager in February 1992 to replace Ossie Ardiles and avert relegation to the old Third Division by a hair's breadth. Not only did he take the club back the top flight as Second Division Champions the following season, aided and abetted by millionaire chairman Sir John Hall, but he assembled an attractive team featuring the England attacking triumvirate of Beardsley, Lee and Ferdinand supplied from the flanks by French winger David Ginola.

The previous season's sale of sharpshooter Andy Cole to rivals Manchester United (with Ulsterman Keith Gillespie moving in part exchange) was looking good business as Newcastle flew high at the top of the table in 1995-96, the Old Trafford outfit trailing 12 points in their wake. The Magpies seemed odds-on to take the title, but were unable to press home their commanding lead. Many critics claimed the rot set in with the addition of £7.5 million Colombian international striker Faustino Asprilla to the forward strength. Beardsley was pushed wide, and four points out of a possible 18 from February onwards told its own story.

Even discounting Asprilla and team-mate Ginola, the Premiership had been an even more exotic place than usual that season. Dutch superstar Ruud Gullit had joined Chelsea on a free transfer from Sampdoria, any saving in fee negated by his colossal wage in a pattern often to be repeated in the post-Bosman era.

Liverpool, with £8.5 million British record signing Stan Collymore in their ranks, had beaten Newcastle 4-3 in what was clearly the most sensational game of the season, but failed to catch the top two and also lost to Manchester United in the FA Cup Final, handing their rivals the Double. Blackburn had suffered a hangover after the sudden early-season departure of Kenny Dalglish from the manager's position—exactly as at Liverpool in 1991. His successor was coach Ray Harford, whose decision to let 31-goal Alan Shearer return to his native Tyneside in July for a British record £15 million seemed to have given the Magpies the initiative to go one better in 1996-97. But it wasn't to be.

George Graham returned to football in September 1996 at Leeds, having spent 18 months in the wilderness after an FA enquiry into illegal payments. Two months later player-coach Gordon Strachan took the reins from Ron Atkinson at Coventry, the pre-arranged handover accelerated due to the Sky Blues' poor form. Ray Harford departed Ewood Park by mutual consent, the club remaining without a permanent manager for the rest of the season: first choice Sven Goran Eriksson decided to stay in Italy and Roy Hodgson was eventually chosen after they finished 13th. Further down the scale outside the Premiership, Bournemouth went into receivership but staved off bankruptcy when a group of local fans bought the club.

Newcastle had thrashed Manchester United 5-0 in October 1996, but there was unrest behind the scenes. Kevin Keegan stepped down with the season scarcely half over, Kenny Dalglish (ironically, the man who replaced him as a player at Liverpool in the 1970s) stepping into his vacated hotseat. The title chase in which his team participated was a hotly contested one as long-time leaders Liverpool, Arsenal, Newcastle and Manchester United all had realistic pretensions. In the end, it was United who clinched it, but had to bid farewell to Eric Cantona after their impetuous French superstar making a decision to retire days before his 31st birthday. Player of the Year was Italian international Gianfranco Zola, whose club Chelsea won the FA Cup.

Since its foundation, the Premiership had mirrored the early days for the Football League which before the advent of the 20th century had been dominated by northern clubs. The 1997-98 campaign was to change all this as Arsenal emerged victorious—but as before they had to come from behind to do it as we have discussed already.

As might be expected, the squad competing for England in the race for the World Cup in France '98 had a good number of players from Arsenal and Manchester United. But it was the number of Premiership players competing for other countries that underlined the fact that England was the place to be seen playing your football. Ironically, Petrescu (Chelsea) and Moldovan (Coventry) scored the goals that put Glenn Hoddle's national team under pressure when they lost to Romania, but defeat did not prove fatal and the English villain was more likely to be perceived as the immature Beckham than the gifted foreign players who graced the French football stage weeks after finishing an arduous Premiership season. England supporters can relax in the koowledge that many more are clamouring to play in the Premiership of 1998-99.

Above: *Paul Merson surprisingly released by Arsenal before the 1997-98 season, has shot relegated Middlesbrough back to the Premiership and retained his England place. Allsport*

League History

League Statistics

1992-93
Champions	Manchester United
Runners-up	Aston Villa
Promoted from Div 1	Newcastle United
	West Ham United
	Swindon Town
Relegated to Div 1	Crystal Palace
	Middlesbrough
	Nottingham Forest

1993-94
Champions	Manchester United
Runners-up	Blackburn Rovers
Promoted from Div 1	Crystal Palace
	Nottingham Forest
	Leicester City
Relegated	Sheffield United
	Oldham Athletic
	Swindon Town

1994-95
Champions	Blackburn Rovers
Runners-up	Manchester United
Promoted from Div 1	Middlesbrough
	Bolton Wanderers
Relegated to Div 1	Crystal Palace
	Norwich City
	Leicester City
	Ipswich Town

1995-96
Champions	Manchester United
Runners-up	Newcastle United
Promoted from Div 1	Sunderland
	Derby County
	Leicester City
Relegated to Div 1	Manchester City
	Queens Park Rangers
	Bolton Wanderers

1996-97
Champions	Manchester United
Runners-up	Newcastle United
Promoted from Div 1	Bolton Wanderers
	Barnsley
	Crystal Palace
Relegated to Div 1	Sunderland
	Middlesbrough
	Nottingham Forest

1997-98
Champions	Arsenal
Runners-up	Manchester United
Promoted from Div 1	Nottingham Forest
	Middlesbrough
	Charlton Athletic
Relegated to Div 1	Bolton Wanderers
	Barnsley
	Crystal Palace

Below: *Manchester United celebrate the '96/97 season triumph.* Allsport

Below: *The Blackburn squad celebrates their '94/95 season victory.* Allsport

Premier League Honours

	Champions	Runners-up
Arsenal	1	—
Aston Villa	—	1
Blackburn Rovers	1	1
Manchester United	4	2
Newcastle United	—	2

Hotshots

Season	Goals	Player	Team
'92-93	22	Teddy Sheringham	Forest/Spurs
'93-94	34	Andy Cole	Newcastle United
'94-95	34	Alan Shearer	Blackburn Rovers
'95-96	31	Alan Shearer	Blackburn Rovers
'96-97	25	Alan Shearer	Newcastle United
'97-98	18	Dion Dublin	Coventry City
	18	Michael Owen	Liverpool
	18	Chris Sutton	Blackburn Rovers

PREMIER LEAGUE FOOTBALL

League Statistics

Final Premiership Table

Team	Pld	W	D	L	F	A	GD	Pts
Arsenal	**38**	**23**	**9**	**6**	**68**	**33**	**35**	**78**
Manchester United	**38**	**23**	**8**	**7**	**73**	**26**	**47**	**77**
Liverpool	38	18	11	9	68	42	26	65
Chelsea	38	20	3	15	71	43	28	63
Leeds United	38	17	8	13	57	46	11	59
Blackburn Rovers	38	16	10	12	57	52	5	58
Aston Villa	38	17	6	15	49	48	1	57
West Ham United	38	16	8	14	56	57	1	56
Derby County	38	16	7	15	52	49	3	55
Leicester City	38	13	14	11	51	41	10	53
Coventry City	38	12	16	10	46	44	2	52
Southampton	38	14	6	18	50	55	-5	48
Newcastle United	38	11	11	16	35	44	-9	44
Tottenham Hotspur	38	11	11	16	44	56	-12	44
Wimbledon	38	10	14	14	34	46	-12	44
Sheffield Wednesday	38	12	8	18	52	67	-15	44
Everton	38	9	13	16	41	56	-15	40
Bolton	**38**	**9**	**13**	**16**	**41**	**61**	**-20**	**40**
Barnsley	**38**	**10**	**5**	**23**	**37**	**82**	**-45**	**35**
Crystal Palace	**38**	**8**	**9**	**21**	**37**	**71**	**-34**	**33**

Right: *Ian Wright proudly holds aloft the Premiershipship Trophy of season 1997/98; however, he spent most of the season on the sidelines with niggling injuries.* Shaun Botterill/Allsport

Next Page: *Andy Cole of Manchester United and Stuart Pearce of Newcastle fight for a high ball.* Allsport

PREMIER LEAGUE FOOTBALL

Statistics

Arsenal

T he sight of Tony Adams blasting the ball left-footed into the back of the Everton net on 3 May 1998 and winning the Premiership for the first time for Arsenal will stay with Gunners' fans for a long time. It may not rank alongside Mickey Thomas's last-minute championship winner against Liverpool in 1988-89, but it did set the seal on a season that did not seem likely to offer much hope for success at the beginning of December. Then, three losses in four games — to Sheffield Wednesday, Liverpool and Blackburn — seemed to have put paid to a season that had started so promisingly.

In the end a fantastic run after Christmas, superb skills from Bergkamp, Anelka and Overmars, crucial goals by Wreh, and a powerhouse French midfield duo in Vieira and Petit, saw the Arsenal home with two games to spare, justifying the club's appointment of quietly-spoken French manager Arsène Wenger and all the expensive purchases that made Arsenal England's mst expensive team.

Although the club may have failed to capture the hearts of football enthusiasts in the same way as, say, Manchester United or Liverpool, they have established themselves since their introduction to the Second Division in 1893 as a club with a great sense of tradition and achievement, and inspire fierce loyalty in their supporters.

In the years leading up to World War I, Woolwich Arsenal, as they remained until their move to north London in 1913, were unspectacular, being relegated for the only time in their history. Since their return to the First Division in 1919, Arsenal have played continuously in the top flight, a record which no other club comes close to equalling.

Under Herbert Chapman the League Championship went to Highbury four seasons out of five in the early 1930s, sandwiched by FA Cup victories in 1930 and 1936, although, curiously, Arsenal never appeared at Wembley in their Championship seasons until their famous Double in 1970-71. Ted Drake, Cliff Bastin, and David Jack were among the players who made this the club's most successful period.

After the war, Arsenal's fortunes waned until the appointment of Bertie Mee as manager. In 1971 the Gunners achieved their historic first League and FA Cup triumph.

Despite three further Wembley appearances, the late 1970s and early 1980s were disappointing, but major success came again after George Graham took over as manager in 1986. His decade in charge brought Arsenal two League Championships and, after a brief spell under Bruce Rioch, the club celebrated its second Double in 1998 with Arsène Wenger at the helm. His success had been built on Graham-laid foundations, with the addition of imported flair players like Overmars, Petit and Vieira.

Above: *Emmanuel Petit.*
Mark Thompson/Allsport

Right: *Tony Adams.*
Stu Forster/Allsport

Season at a Glance

1997-98 Final Position: Premiership winners
Top League Goalscorers: Bergkamp: 16, Overmars: 12, Wright: 10
Highest League win: 5-0 v Barnsley (H), 4 October 1997
5-0 v Wimbledon (H), 18 April 1998
Worst League Defeat: 0-4 v Liverpool (A), 6 May 1998
Highest Attendance: 38,269 v Everton, 3 May 1998
Lowest Attendance: 37,324 v Coventry City, 11 August 1997

Arsenal

Managers

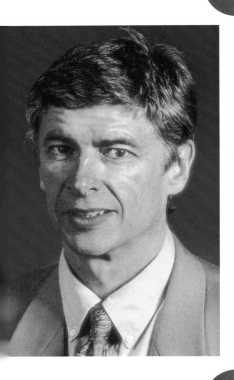

Thomas Mitchell	1897-98
George Elcoat	1898-99
Harry Bradshaw	1899-1904
Phil Kelso	1904-08
George Morrell	1908-15
Leslie Knighton	1919-25
Herbert Chapman	1925-34
George Allison	1934-47
Tom Whittaker	1947-56
Jack Crayston	1956-58
George Swindin	1958-62
Billy Wright	1962-66
Bertie Mee	1966-76
Terry Neill	1976-83
Don Howe	1983-86
George Graham	1986-95
Bruce Rioch	1995-96
Arsène Wenger	1996-

Above: *Manager Arsène Wenger.*
Phil Cole/Allsport

Honours

Premier League Champions:	1997-98 (Double)
Division One Champions:	1930-31, 1932-33, 1933-34, 1934-35, 1937-38, 1947-48, 1952-53, 1970-71 (Double), 1988-89, 1990-91,
Runners-up:	1925-26, 1931-32, 1972-73
Division Two Runners-up:	1903-04
FA Cup Winners:	1930, 1936, 1950, 1971 (Double), 1979, 1993, 1998 (Double)
Runners-up:	1927, 1932, 1952, 1972, 1978, 1980
Football League Cup Winners:	1987, 1993
Runners-up:	1968, 1969, 1988
European Fairs (UEFA) Cup Winners:	1970
Cup Winners' Cup Winners:	1994
Runners-up:	1980, 1995

Club Details

Year formed:	1886
Ground:	Arsenal Stadium, Highbury, London N5 1BU
Nickname:	The Gunners
Club Colours:	Red and white
Manager:	Arsène Wenger
Record attendance:	73,295 v Sunderland, 9 March 1935, Division One
Record League victory:	12-0 v Loughborough Town, 12 March 1900, Division Two – Scorers: Gaudie 3, Dick 2, Cottrell 2, Main 2, Tennant 2, Anderson
Record Cup victory:	11-1 v Darwen, 9 January 1932, FA Cup Third Round – Scorers: Bastin 4, Jack 3, Hulme 2, Lambert 2
Record defeat:	0-8 v Loughborough Town, 12 December 1896, Division One; 0-7 v Aston Villa, 27 December 1930
Highest League scorer in a season:	Ted Drake, 42, 1934-35, Division One
Highest League scorer during career:	Cliff Bastin, 150, 1930-47
Most League appearances:	David O'Leary, 558, 1975-93

Left: *David Seaman.*
Stu Forster/Allsport

97/98 Results

August

9	Leeds United	A	D	1-1	Wright 35
11	Coventry City	H	W	2-0	Wright 29, 47
23	Southampton	A	W	3-1	Overmars 20, Bergkamp 57, 79
27	Leicester City	A	D	3-3	Bergkamp 9, 61 90
30	Tottenham Hotspur	H	D	0-0	

September

13	Bolton Wanderers	H	W	4-1	Wright 20, 25, 81, Parlour 44
16	PAOK Saloniki (UEFA 1-1)	A	L	0-1	
21	Chelsea	A	W	3-2	Bergkamp 45, 59, Winterburn 89
23	West Ham United	H	W	4-0	Bergkamp 12, Overmars 39, 45, Wright 42 (pen)
27	Everton	A	D	2-2	Wright 32, Overmars 41
30	PAOK Saloniki (UEFA 1-2)	H	D	1-1	Bergkamp 22

Dennis Bergkamp.
Stu Forster/Allsport

October

4	Barnsley	H	W	5-0	Bergkamp 25, 32, Parlour 45, Platt 63, Wright 76
14	Birmingham City (CCC 3)	H	W	4-1	Boa Morte 62, 108, Platt 99 (pen), Mendez 113
18	Crystal Palace	A	D	0-0	
26	Aston Villa	H	D	0-0	

November

1	Derby County	A	L	0-3	
9	Manchester United	H	W	3-2	Anelka 7, Vieira 27, Platt 83
18	Coventry City (CCC 4)	H	W	1-0	Bergkamp 99
22	Sheffield Wednesday	A	L	0-2	
30	Liverpool	H	L	0-1	

December

6	Newcastle United	A	W	1-0	Wright 36
13	Blackburn Rovers	H	L	1-3	Overmars 18
26	Leicester City	H	W	2-1	Platt 36, Walsh 56 og
28	Tottenham Hotspur	A	D	1-1	Parlour 62

January

3	Port Vale (FAC 3)	H	D	0-0	
6	West Ham United (CCC QF)	A	W	2-1	Wright 25, Overmars 52
10	Leeds United	H	W	2-1	Overmars 60, 72
14	Port Vale (FAC 3R)	A	W	1-1	Bergkamp 100
	(Won 4-3 on penalties)				
17	Coventry City	A	D	2-2	Bergkamp 50, Anelka 57
24	Middlesbrough (FAC 4)	A	W	2-1	Overmars 2, Parlour 19
28	Chelsea (CCC SF-1)	H	W	2-1	Overmars 23, Hughes 47
31	Southampton	H	W	3-0	Bergkamp 62, Adams 67, Anelka 67

February

8	Chelsea	H	W	2-0	Hughes 4, 42
15	Crystal Palace (FAC 5)	H	D	0-0	
18	Chelsea (CCC SF-2)	A	L	1-3	Bergkamp 82 (pen)
21	Crystal Palace	H	W	1-0	Grimandi 49

March

2	West Ham United	A	D	0-0	
8	West Ham United (FAC 6)	H	D	1-1	Bergkamp 26 (pen)
11	Wimbledon	A	W	1-0	Wreh 21
14	Manchester United	A	W	1-0	Overmars 79
17	West Ham United (FAC 6R)	A	W	1-1	Anelka 45
	(Won 4-3 on penalties)				
28	Sheffield Wednesday	H	W	1-0	Bergkamp 35
31	Bolton Wanderers	A	W	1-0	Wreh 47

April

5	Wolves (FAC SF)	A	W	1-0	Wreh 12
11	Newcastle United	H	W	3-1	Anelka 41, 64, Vieira 72
13	Blackburn Rovers	A	W	4-1	Bergkamp 2, Parlour 7, 14, Anelka 42
18	Wimbledon	H	W	5-0	Adams 12, Overmars 17, Bergkamp 19, Petit 59, Wreh 68
25	Barnsley	A	W	2-0	Bergkamp 23, Overmars 76
29	Derby County	H	W	1-0	Petit 34

May

3	Everton	H	W	4-0	Bilic 6 og, Overmars 28, 57, Adams 89
6	Liverpool	A	L	0-4	
10	Aston Villa	A	L	0-1	
16	Newcastle United (FAC F)		W	2-0	Overmars 23, Anelka 69

Patrick Vieira.
Stu Forster/Allsport

PREMIER LEAGUE FOOTBALL

Squad

GOALKEEPERS
DAVID SEAMAN
ALEX MANNINGER
JOHN LUKIC

DEFENDERS
LEE DIXON   STEVE BOULD   TONY ADAMS   NIGEL WINTERBURN
ALBERTO MENDEZ   MARTIN KEOWN   GILLES GRIMANDI   MATTHEW UPSON
DAVID GRODIN

MIDFIELDERS
RAY PARLOUR   REMI GARDE   PATRICK VIEIRA   MARC OVERMARS
LUIS BOA MORTE   EMMANUEL PETIT   STEPHEN HUGHES   JASON CROWE

STRIKERS
CHRISTOPHER WREH
DENNIS BERGKAMP   NICOLAS ANELKA   ISAIH RANKIN

Tony Adams
DOB: 10/10/66, Romford
Signed: Apprentice, January 1984
League Debut: 5/11/83

Nicolas Anelka
DOB: 14/3/79, Versailles, France
Signed: Paris St Germain, February 1997
League Debut: 5/4/97

Dennis Bergkamp
DOB: 18/5/69, Amsterdam, Holland
Signed: Inter Milan, (£7.5 million) July 1995
League Debut: 20/8/95

Michael Black
DOB: 6/10/76, Chigwell
Signed: Trainee, June 1993
League Debut: TBA

Luis Boa Morte Pereira
DOB: 4/8/78, Lisbon, Portugal
Signed: Sporting Lisbon, (£1.75 million) June 1997
League Debut: 23/8/97

Steve Bould
DOB: 16/11/62, Stoke-on-Trent
Signed: Stoke City, (£390,000) June 1988
League Debut: 27/8/88

Lee Dixon
DOB: 17/3/64, Manchester
Signed: Stoke City, (£350,000) January 1988
League Debut: 13/2/88

Remi Garde
DOB: 3/4/66, L'Arbresle, France
Signed: Racing Strasbourg, (free) August 1996
League Debut: 26/10/96 v Leeds

Gilles Grimandi
DOB: 11/11/70, Gap, Grance
Signed: AS Monaco, (£2 million) June 1997
League Debut: 9/8/97

Stephen Hughes
DOB: 18/9/76, Wokingham
Signed: Apprentice, July 1995
League Debut: 26/12/94

Martin Keown
DOB: 24/7/66, Oxford
Signed: Everton, (£2 million) February 1993
League Debut: 23/11/85

John Lukic
DOB: 11/12/60, Chesterfield
Signed: Leeds United, July 1983
League Debut: 7/4/84

Alex Manninger
DOB: 4/6/77, Salzburg, Austria
Signed: Casino Graz, (£500,000) June 1997
League Debut: 31/1/98

Alberto Mendez
DOB: 24/10/74, Numberg, Germany
Signed: FC Feucht, (£250,000) June 1997
League Debut: 18/10/97

Marc Overmars
DOB: 29/3/73, Emst, Holland
Signed: Ajax, (undisclosed) June 1997
League Debut: 9/8/97

Ray Parlour
DOB: 7/3/73, Romford
Signed: Apprentice, March 1991
League Debut: 29/1/92

Emmanuel Petit
DOB: 22/9/70, Dieppe, France
Signed: AS Monaco, (£3 million) June 1997
League Debut: 9/8/97

David Seaman
DOB: 19/9/63, Rotherham
Signed: Queens Park Rangers, (£1.3m), May 1990
League Debut: 25/8/90

Matthew Upson
DOB: 18/4/79, Hartismere
Signed: Luton Town, (£1.2 million) May 1997
League Debut: 17/1/98

Patrick Vieira
DOB: 23/6/76, Dakar, Senegal
Signed: AC Milan, (£4 million) August 1996
League Debut: 16/9/96

Nigel Winterburn
DOB: 11/12/63, Nuneaton
Signed: Wimbledon, (£350,000) May 1987
League Debut: 21/11/87

Christopher Wreh
DOB: 14/5/75, Monrovia, Liberia
Signed: AS Monaco, (£300,000) August 1997
League Debut: 1/11/97

1998-99 Premier League Fixtures

	Home	Away			Home	Away
Aston Villa	16 May	12 Dec	Liverpool		9 Jan	22 Aug
Blackburn Rovers	5 Apr	24 Oct	Manchester United		19 Sep	13 Feb
Charlton Athletic	29 Aug	28 Dec	Middlesbrough		28 Nov	24 Apr
Chelsea	30 Jan	9 Sep	Newcastle United		3 Oct	27 Feb
Coventry City	20 Mar	31 Oct	Nottingham Forest		15 Aug	16 Jan
Derby County	1 May	5 Dec	Sheffield Wednesday		6 Mar	26 Sep
Everton	7 Nov	13 Mar	Southampton		17 Oct	3 Apr
Leeds United	19 Dec	8 May	Tottenham Hotspur		14 Nov	10 Apr
Leicester City	20 Feb	12 Sep	West Ham United		26 Dec	6 Feb
			Wimbledon		17 Apr	21 Nov

Left: *Marc Overmars.* Ben Radford/ Allsport

Below: *Ian Wright celebrates breaking Cliff Basten's all games' goal scoring record with his 179th goal.* Allsport

Transfers In: David Grondin (St Etienne £500,00)
Tranfers Out: Ian Wright (West Ham £750,000), Scot Marshall (Southampton free), David Platt (retired)

PREMIER LEAGUE FOOTBALL

Manchester Utd

Above: *New signing Jaap Stam.*
Alex Livesey/Allsport

Right: *David Beckham.*
Shaun Botterill/Allsport

The best team of the 1990s, Manchester United's name has become synonymous with success. Despite the loss of Roy Keane to injury, the 1997-98 season started like a re-run of what had gone before. Up to Christmas 16 wins—including 7–0 and 6–1 drubbings of Barnsley and Sheffield Wednesday respectively, and comfortable victories against FC Kosice (twice) and Feyenoord that put them through to the knock-out stages of the European Champions' League—seemed to indicate that it was business as usual. The only loss had been by the odd goal in a five-goal thriller at Highbury.

Then, for United fans, everything seemed to go wrong. Against Juve they could not turn superiority into victory and let the Italians—the eventual winners of the League—stay in the competition with a 2–1 victory. At home, Man U were on the wrong side of another five-goaler against Coventry and then lost twice by the smallest possible margin away to Southampton and Leicester City. Another loss to Arsenal, this time in front of the Old Trafford faithful, a 2–3 loss to an inspired Barnsley in the FA Cup, and a wafer-thin loss to Monaco by the away goal in the Champions' League and the season was as good as over. The eventual difference in the Championship, a solitary point just rubbed salt in the wounds. But, of course, there was Beckham to look forward to in the World Cup . . .

The road to glory has been far from smooth for United, and for many years after joining an enlarged First Division in 1892 they struggled to survive and spent long periods period in Division Two. They started the postwar period under a new manager, the legendary Matt Busby. It is largely due to his charisma and skill that United enjoy their current reputation. The mid-1950s saw the world-famous 'Busby Babes', including Bobby Charlton, Roger Byrne and the immensely talented Duncan Edwards. These phenomenal youngsters brought two Championships to Old Trafford and threatened to dominate English football but the tragedy of the Munich air crash in February 1958 left behind broken dreams. Incredibly Busby succeeded in building another magnificent side: Bobby Charlton, Denis Law and George Best were among the United greats of the 1960s, a team which became the first English club to lift the European Cup in 1968.

After Sir Matt, the Red Devils experienced mixed fortunes until the arrival of Alex Ferguson in November 1986, although it was five years before his spending began to yield results. They were the Premiership's first title holders in 1992-93 and went one better by completing the Double a year later. Since then, they have worn the crown twice more, achieving the double Double in 1996, with Giggs, Beckham, Scholes, the Neville brothers and Schmeichel writing their names into Old Trafford history. There's no doubt that, with Roy Keane back, Man U will be challenging again in 1998-99.

Season at a Glance

1997-98 Final Position:	Finished second in the Premiership
Top League Goalscorers:	Cole: 16, Beckham: 9, Sheringham: 9
Highest League win:	7-0 v Barnsley (H), 25 October 1997
Worst League Defeat:	2-3 v Arsenal (A), 9 November 1997
	2-3 v Coventry City (A), 28 December 1997
Highest Attendance:	55,306 v Wimbledon, 28 March 1998
Lowest Attendance:	55,008 v Southampton, 13 August 1997

PREMIER LEAGUE FOOTBALL

Manchester Utd

Managers

Ernest Mangnall	1903-12
John Robson	1914-21
John Chapman	1921-26
Clarence Hilditch	1926-27
Herbert Bamlett	1927-31
Archie Scott Duncan	1932-37
Matt Busby	1945-69
Wilf McGuinness	1969-70
Sir Matt Busby	1970-71
Frank O'Farrell	1971-72
Tommy Docherty	1972-77
Dave Sexton	1977-81
Ron Atkinson	1981-86
Alex Ferguson	1986-

Manager Alex Ferguson.
Gary M. Prior/Allsport

Honours

Premier League Champions:	1992-93, 1993-94 (Double), 1995-96 (Double), 1996-97
Runners-up:	1994-95, 1997-98
Division One Champions:	1907-08, 1910-11, 1951-52, 1955-56, 1956-57, 1964-65, 1966-67
Runners-up:	1946-47, 1947-48, 1948-49, 1950-51, 1958-59, 1963-64, 1967-68, 1979-80, 1987-88, 1991-92
Division Two Champions:	1935-36, 1974-75
Runners-up:	1896-97, 1905-06, 1924-25, 1937-38
FA Cup Winners:	1909, 1948, 1963, 1977, 1983, 1985, 1990,1994 (Double), 1996 (Double),
Runners-up:	1957, 1958, 1976, 1979, 1995
Football League Cup Winners:	1992
Runners-up:	1983, 1991, 199
European Cup Winners:	1967-68
Cup Winners' Cup Winners:	1990-91
World Club Championship Runners-up:	1968
Super Cup Winners:	1991

Club Details

Year formed:	1878
Ground:	Old Trafford, Manchester M16 0RA
Nickname:	The Red Devils
Club Colours:	Red, white and black
Manager:	Alex Ferguson

Record attendance:
70,504 v Aston Villa, 27 December 1920, Division One

Record League victory:
10-1 v Wolverhampton Wanderers, 15 October 1892, Division One – Scorers: Stewart 3, Donaldson 3, Farman, Hood, Carson, Hendry

Record Cup victory:
10-0 v RSC Anderlecht, 26 September 1956, European Cup preliminary round second leg – Scorers: Viollet 4, Taylor 3, Whelan 2, Berry

Record defeat:
0-7 v Blackburn, 10 Apr 26; v Aston Villa 27 Dec 30; v Wolves 26 Dec 31

Highest League scorer in a season:
Dennis Viollet, 32, 1959-60, Division One

Highest League scorer during career:
Bobby Charlton, 199, 1956-73

Most League appearances:
Bobby Charlton, 606, 1956-73

Peter Schmeichel.
Ben Radford/Allsport

97/98 Results

August

3	Chelsea (CS)		W	1-1	Johnsen 57
					(4-2 on penalties)
10	Tottenham Hotspur	A	W	2-0	Butt 82, Vega 83 og
13	Southampton	H	W	1-0	Beckham 78
23	Leicester City	A	D	0-0	
27	Everton	A	W	2-0	Beckham 29, Sheringham 51
30	Coventry City	H	W	3-0	Cole 2, Keane 72, Poborsky 90

September

13	West Ham United	H	W	2-1	Keane 21, Scholes 76
17	FC Kosice (ECL)	A	W	3-0	Irwin 29, Berg 60, Cole 88
20	Bolton Wanderers	A	D	0-0	
24	Chelsea	H	D	2-2	Scholes 36, Solskjaer 86
27	Leeds United	A	L	0-1	

October

1	Juventus (ECL)	H	W	3-2	Sheringham 38, Scholes 69, Giggs 89
4	Crystal Palace	H	W	2-0	Sheringham 17, Hreidarsson 30 og
15	Ipswich Town (CCC 3)	A	L	0-2	
18	Derby County	A	D	2-2	Sheringham 51, Cole 84
22	Feyenoord (ECL)	H	W	2-1	Scholes 32, Irwin 72 (pen)
25	Barnsley	H	W	7-0	Cole 17, 19, 45, Giggs 43, 56, Scholes 59, Poborsky 80

November

1	Sheffield Wednesday	H	W	6-1	Sheringham 13, 63, Cole 20, 38, Solskjaer 41, 75
5	Feyenoord (ECL)	A	W	3-1	Cole 31, 44, 73
9	Arsenal	A	L	2-3	Sheringham 33, 41
22	Wimbledon	A	W	5-2	Butt 48, Beckham 66, 76, Scholes 81, Cole 87
27	FC Kosice (ECL)	H	W	3-0	Cole 40, Faktor 85 og, Sheringham 90
30	Blackburn Rovers	H	W	4-0	Solskjaer 18, 53, Henchoz 60 og, Kenna 85 og

Andy Cole.
Shaun Botterill/Allsport

December

6	Liverpool	A	W	3-1	Cole 51, 74, Beckham 70
10	Juventus (ECL)	A	L	0-1	
15	Aston Villa	H	W	1-0	Giggs 52
21	Newcastle United	A	W	1-0	Cole 66
26	Everton	H	W	2-0	Berg 14, Cole 35
28	Coventry City	A	L	2-3	Solskjaer 30, Sheringham 47

January

4	Chelsea (FAC 3)	A	W	5-3	Beckham 23, 28, Cole 45, 65, Sheringham 74
10	Tottenham Hotspur	H	W	2-0	Giggs 44, 67
19	Southampton	A	L	0-1	
24	Walsall (FAC 4)	H	W	5-1	Cole 10, 65, Solskjaer 39, 69, Johnsen 74
31	Leicester City	H	L	0-1	

February

7	Bolton Wanderers	H	D	1-1	Cole 85
15	Barnsley (FAC 5)	H	D	1-1	Sheringham 42
18	Aston Villa	A	W	2-0	Beckham 82, Giggs 89
21	Derby County	H	W	2-0	Giggs 18, Irwin 71 (pen)
25	Barnsley (FAC 5R)	A	L	2-3	Sheringham 56, Cole 82
28	Chelsea	A	W	1-0	P Neville 31

March

4	Monaco (EC Q-F)	A	D	0-0	
7	Sheffield Wednesday	A	L	0-2	
11	West Ham United	A	D	1-1	Scholes 67
14	Arsenal	H	L	0-1	
18	Monaco (EC Q-F)	H	D	1-1	Solskjaer 53
28	Wimbledon	H	W	2-0	Johnsen 83, Scholes 90

April

6	Blackburn Rovers	A	W	3-1	Cole 56, Scholes 73, Beckham 89
10	Liverpool	H	D	1-1	Johnsen 13
18	Newcastle United	H	D	1-1	Beckham 38
27	Crystal Palace	A	W	3-0	Scholes 5, Butt 21, Cole 84

May

4	Leeds United	H	W	3-0	Giggs 6, Irwin 29 (pen), Beckham 59
10	Barnsley	A	W	2-0	Cole 5, Sheringham 67

Paul Scholes.
Mark Thompson/Allsport

PREMIER LEAGUE FOOTBALL

Manchester Utd

Squad

GOALKEEPERS
PETER SCHMEICHEL
RAIMOND VAN DER GOUW

DEFENDERS
HENNING BERG   RONNIE JOHNSEN   DAVID MAY   DENIS IRWIN
GARY NEVILLE   JAAP STAM   PHIL NEVILLE   JOHN CURTIS
MICHAEL CLEGG   RONNIE WALLWORK

MIDFIELDERS
DAVID BECKHAM   NICKY BUTT   ROY KEANE   JORDI CRUYFF
PAUL SCHOLES   RYAN GIGGS

STRIKERS
ANDY COLE
TEDDY SHERINGHAM   OLE GUNNAR SOLSKJAER
ERIK NEVLAND

David Beckham
DOB: 2/5/75, Leytonstone
Signed: Trainee, January 1993
League Debut: 2/4/95

Henning Berg
DOB: 1/9/68, Eidsvoll, Norway
Signed: Blackburn Rovers,
(£5 million) 1997
League Debut: 13/8/97

Nicky Butt
DOB: 21/1/75, Manchester
Signed: Trainee, January 1993
League Debut: 21/11/92

Andy Cole
DOB: 15/10/71, Nottingham
Signed: Newcastle United,
(£6 million) January 1995
League Debut: 22/1/95

Jordi Cruyff
DOB: 9/2/74, Amsterdam, Holland
Signed: Barcelona, 1996
League Debut: 17/8/96

John Curtis
DOB: 3/9/78, Nuneaton
Signed: Trainee
League Debut: 25/10/87

Ryan Giggs
DOB: 29/11/73, Cardiff
Signed: Trainee, November 1990
League Debut: 2/3/91

Denis Irwin
DOB: 31/10/65, Cork, Eire
Signed: Oldham Athletic,
(£650,000) June 1990
League Debut: 25/8/90

Ronnie Johnsen
DOB: 10/6/69, Sandefjord,
Norway
Signed: Besiktas, (£1.5 million)
July 1996
League Debut: 17/8/96

Roy Keane
DOB: 10/8/71, Cork, Eire
Signed: Nottingham Forest,
(£3.75 million) July 1993
League Debut: 15/8/93

David May
DOB: 24/6/70, Oldham
Signed: Blackburn Rovers, (£1.4
million) July 1994
League Debut: 20/8/94

Gary Neville
DOB:18/2/75, Bury
Signed: Trainee, January 1993
League Debut: 8/5/94

Phil Neville
DOB: 21/1/77, Bury
Signed: Trainee, June 1994
League Debut: 11/2/95

Peter Schmeichel
DOB: 18/11/63, Gladsaxe,
Denmark
Signed: Brondby IF, (£550,000)
August 1991
League Debut: 17/8/91

Paul Scholes
DOB: 16/11/74, Salford
Signed: Trainee, January 1993
League Debut: 24/9/94

Teddy Sheringham
DOB: 2/4/66, Highams Park
Signed: Tottenham Hotspur,
(£3.5 million) July 1997
League Debut: 10/8/97

Ole Gunnar Solskjaer
DOB: 26/2/73, Kristiansund,
Norway
Signed: Molde, (£1.5 million)
July 1996
League Debut: 25/8/96

Jaap Stam
DOB: 17/7/72, Holland
Signed: PSV Eindhoven,
(£10.75 million) May 1998
League Debut: TBA

Raimond Van Der Gouw
DOB: 24/3/63, Oldenzaal,
Holland
Signed: Vitesse, 1996
League Debut: 23/11/96

1998-99 Premier League Fixtures

	Home	Away		Home	Away
Arsenal	13 Feb	19 Sep	Liverpool	26 Sep	6 Mar
Aston Villa	1 May	5 Dec	Middlesbrough	19 Dec	8 May
Blackburn Rovers	14 Nov	10 Apr	Newcastle United	7 Nov	13 Mar
Charlton Athletic	30 Jan	8 Sep	Nottingham Forest	26 Dec	6 Feb
Chelsea	23 Sep	28 Dec	Sheffield Wednesday	17 Apr	21 Nov
Coventry City	12 Sep	20 Feb	Southampton	27 Feb	3 Oct
Derby County	5 Apr	24 Oct	Tottenham Hotspur	16 May	12 Dec
Everton	20 Mar	31 Oct	West Ham United	9 Jan	22 Aug
Leeds United	28 Nov	24 Apr	Wimbledon	17 Oct	3 Apr
Leicester City	15 Aug	16 Jan			

Left: *Ryan Giggs.*
Ben Radford/
Allsport

Below:
*Manchester
United before the
3–0 victory over
Kosice, 27
November 1997.*
Mark Thompson/
Allsport

Transfers In: Jaap Stam (PSV £10.5m), Jesper Blomqvist
(Parma £5m)

Tranfers Out: Gary Pallister (Middlesbrough £2.5m), Brian McClair (Motherwell free), Ben
Thornley (Huddesfield tribunal)

Manchester Utd

Liverpool

The most successful English club of all time, in recent seasons Liverpool has flattered to deceive. Despite a string of household names such as Ince, McManaman, Redknapp, and Fowler, the 1997-98 season expired leaving Liverpool a massive 12 points behind second place Man U. There were flashes of brilliance, but two wins in the league against Arsenal—including a satisfying 4–1 thrashing the week after the London side lifted the Premiership trophy—and the arrival of a young striker called Michael Owen (and a small matter of his 18 Premiership goals) could not hide a porous defence, and less than satisfactory performances from a side that should have delivered more. The season was summed up by a supine 3–0 away loss to Strasbourg in the EUFA Cup that no amount of heroics in the home leg could dispel.

Then came the World Cup and that wonderful goal by Michael Owen, who looked every inch a world beater when he got onto the field. He may not win the Reds the '98-99 Premiership, but a strengthened squad sees Steve Staunton return from Villa, Sean Dundee arrive from Karlsruhe, and a Frenchman sitting alongside Roy Evans in the dugout. Perhaps there will be something to shout about . . .

Liverpool's story began unremarkably enough when they joined the Second Division in 1893 and displayed erratic form throughout much of their first 60 years, five League Championships interspersed with many disappointing seasons and, in 1954, the drop to the Second Division. The arrival of Bill Shankly as manager in 1959 marked the beginning of the Liverpool renaissance, and since regaining their First Division status in 1962 the Anfield club has never looked back. He transformed a mediocre side, and his passion rubbed off on all who worked with him. Under his leadership, Liverpool took three League titles, put their name on the FA Cup for the first time, and in 1972 began a remarkable 19-season run in which they only once finished lower than third in the First Division.

Shankly shook Liverpool by retiring unexpectedly in 1974, but former back-room boy Bob Paisley stepped into the limelight and the first of their four European Cup wins came in 1977. The League Championship seemed to reside permanently at Anfield, and the League Cup went there on four successive occasions in 1981-84. Key players included Kenny Dalglish and Graeme Souness, both later Liverpool managers, and Alan Hansen.

Paisley resigned in 1983, but the Liverpool juggernaut rolled on, guided first by Joe Fagan and then Dalglish, whose surprise resignation in 1991 rocked the club. Though Graeme Souness brought the FA Cup to Anfield in 1992, their players were past their peak and it fell to Roy Evans to rebuild the side. The sustained Championship challenge craved for by supporters, who have never seen Premiership success, remains long overdue.

Above: *Paul Ince.*
Gary M. Prior/Allsport

Right: *Michael Owen.*
Clive Brunskill/Allsport

Season at a Glance

1997-98 Final Position:	3rd in the Premiership
Top League Goalscorers:	Owen: 18, McManaman: 11, Fowler: 9
Highest League win:	5-0 v West Ham United (H), 2 May 1998
Worst League Defeat:	1-4 v Chelsea (A), 25 April 1998
Highest Attendance:	44,532 v Bolton, 7 March 1998
Lowest Attendance:	34,705 v Sheffield Wed, 13 September 1997

Liverpool

Managers

Above: *Roy Evans.*
L. Griffiths/Allsport

John McKenna	1892-96
Tom Watson	1896-1915
David Ashworth	1919-23
Matt McQueen	1923-28
George Patterson	1928-36
George Kay	1936-51
Don Welsh	1951-56
Phil Taylor	1956-59
Bill Shankly	1959-74
Bob Paisley	1974-83
Joe Fagan	1983-85
Kenny Dalglish	1985-91
Graeme Souness	1991-94
Roy Evans	1994-
Joint manager with Gerard Houllier	1998-

Honours

Division One Champions:	1900-01, 1905-06, 1921-22, 1922-23, 1946-47, 1963-64, 1965-66, 1972-73, 1975-76, 1976-77, 1978-79, 1979-80, 1981-82, 1982-83, 1983-84, 1985-86 (Double), 1987-88, 1989-90
Runners-up:	1898-99, 1909-10, 1968-69, 1973-74, 1974-75, 1977-78, 1984-85, 1986-87, 1988-89, 1990-91
FA Cup Winners:	1965, 1974, 1986 (Double), 1992
Runners-up:	1914, 1950, 1971, 1977, 1988, 1996
Football League Cup Winners:	1981, 1982, 1983, 1984, 1995
Runners-up:	1978, 1987
League Super Cup Winners:	1986
European Cup Winners:	1977, 1978, 1981, 1984
Runners-up:	1985
European Cup Winners' Cup Runners-up:	1966
UEFA Cup Winners:	1973, 1976
European Super Cup Winners:	1977
World Club Championship Runners-up:	1981

46

Club Details

Year formed:	1892
Ground:	Anfield Road, Liverpool L4 0TH
Nickname:	The Reds or Pool
Club Colours:	Red
Managers:	Roy Evans and Gerard Houllier

Record attendance: 61,905 v Wolverhampton Wanderers, 2 February 1952, FA Cup Fourth Round

Record League victory: 10-1 v Rotherham Town, 18 February 1896, Division Two – Scorers: Allan 4, McVean 3, Ross 2, Becton

Record Cup victory: 11-0 v Stromsgodset Drammen,17 September 1974, European Cup Winners' Cup First Round first leg – Scorers: Thompson 2, Boersma 2, Smith, Lindsay (pen), Cormack, Hughes, Heighway, Kennedy, Callaghan

Record defeat: 1-9 v Birmingham City, 11 December 1954, Division Two

Highest League scorer in a season: Roger Hunt, 41, 1961-62, Division Two
Highest League scorer during career: Roger Hunt, 245, 1959-69
Most League appearances: Ian Callaghan, 640, 1960-78

Phil Babb.
Ben Radford/Allsport

Liverpool

97/98 Results

August

9	Wimbledon	A	D	1-1	Owen 71 (pen)
13	Leicester City	H	L	1-2	Ince 85
23	Blackburn Rovers	A	D	1-1	Owen 52
26	Leeds United	A	W	2-0	McManaman 23, Riedle 75

September

13	Sheffield Wednesday	H	W	2-1	Ince 55, Thomas 68
16	Celtic (UEFA 1-1)	A	D	2-2	Owen 6, McManaman 89
20	Southampton	A	D	1-1	Riedle 37
22	Aston Villa	H	W	3-0	Fowler 56 (pen), McManaman 79, Riedle 90
27	West Ham United	A	L	1-2	Fowler 52
30	Celtic (UEFA 1-2)	H	D	0-0	

October

5	Chelsea	H	W	4-2	Berger 20, 35, 57, Fowler 64
15	West Brom (CCC 3)	A	W	2-0	Berger 52, Fowler 89
18	Everton	A	L	0-2	
21	RC Strasbourg (UEFA 2-1)	A	L	0-3	
25	Derby County	H	W	4-0	Fowler 27, 84, Leonhardsen 65, McManaman 88

Steve Staunton.
Phil Cole/Allsport

November

1	Bolton Wanderers	A	D	1-1	Fowler 1
4	RC Strasbourg (UEFA 2-2)	H	W	2-0	Fowler 63 (pen), Riedle 84
8	Tottenham Hotspur	H	W	4-0	McManaman 48, Leonhardsen 50, Redknapp 65, Owen 86
18	Grimsby Town (CCC 4)	H	W	3-0	Owen 28, 45 (pen), 57
22	Barnsley	H	L	0-1	
30	Arsenal	A	W	1-0	McManaman 55

December

6	Manchester United	H	L	1-3	Fowler 60 (pen)
13	Crystal Palace	A	W	3-0	McManaman 39, Owen 56, Leonhardsen 61
20	Coventry City	H	W	1-0	Owen 14
26	Leeds United	H	W	3-1	Owen 46, Fowler 79, 83
28	Newcastle United	A	W	2-1	McManaman 31, 43

January

3	Coventry City (FAC 3)	H	L	1-3	Redknapp 7
7	Newcastle United (CCC QF)	A	W	2-0	Owen 95, Fowler 103
10	Wimbledon	H	W	2-0	Redknapp 71, 84
17	Leicester City	A	D	0-0	
20	Newcastle United	H	W	1-0	Owen 17
27	Middlesbrough (CCC SF-1)	H	W	2-1	Redknapp 31, Fowler 82
31	Blackburn Rovers	H	D	0-0	

February

7	Southampton	H	L	2-3	Owen 24, 90
14	Sheffield Wed'day	A	D	3-3	Owen 27, 73, 78
18	Middlesbrough (CCC SF-2)	A	L	0-2	
23	Everton	H	D	1-1	Ince 66
28	Aston Villa	A	L	1-2	Owen 6 (pen)

March

7	Bolton Wanderers	H	W	2-1	Ince 58, Owen 65
14	Tottenham Hotspur	A	D	3-3	McManaman 21, 89, Ince 64
28	Barnsley	A	W	3-2	Riedle 44, 59, McManaman 90

April

10	Manchester United	A	D	1-1	Owen 36
13	Crystal Palace	H	W	2-1	Leonhardsen 29, Thompson 85
19	Coventry City	A	D	1-1	Owen 33
25	Chelsea	A	L	1-4	Riedle 45

May

2	West Ham United	H	W	5-0	Owen 4, McAteer 21, 25, Leonhardsen 45, Ince 61
6	Arsenal	H	W	4-0	Ince 27, 30, Owen 41, Leonhardsen 87
10	Derby County	A	L	0-1	

Steve McManaman.
Clive Brunskill/Allsport

PREMIER LEAGUE FOOTBALL

Liverpool

Squad

GOALKEEPERS
DAVID JAMES
BRAD FRIEDEL

DEFENDERS
ROB JONES   PHIL BABB   JAMIE CARRAGHER   STIG INGE BJORNEBYE
JASON MCATEER   BJORN TORE KVARME   DOMINIC MATTEO   STEVE HARKNESS
MARK WRIGHT   STEVE STAUNTON

MIDFIELDERS
STEVE MCMANAMAN   PAUL INCE   DANNY MURPHY   OYVIND LEONHARDSEN
JAMIE REDKNAPP   CARL SERRANT   DAVID THOMPSON

STRIKERS
PATRIK BERGER
SEAN DUNDEE   ROBBIE FOWLER   MICHAEL OWEN
KARLHEINZ RIEDLE

Phil Babb
DOB: 30/11/70, Lambeth, London
Signed: Coventry City,
(£3.6 million) September 1994
League Debut: 10/9/94

Patrik Berger
DOB: 10/11/73, Prague, Czech
Republic
Signed: Borussia Dortmund, 1996
League Debut: 7/9/96

Stig Inge Bjornebye
DOB: 11/12/69, Elverum, Norway
Signed: Rosenborg, (£600,000)
December 1992
League Debut: 19/12/92

Jamie Carragher
DOB: 28/1/78, Bootle
Signed: Trainee
League Debut: 11/1/97

Sean Dundee
DOB: 7/12/72, South Africa
Signed: Karlsruhe, May 1998
League Debut: TBA

Robbie Fowler
DOB: 9/4/75, Liverpool
Signed: Trainee, April 1992
League Debut: 25/9/93

Brad Friedel
DOB: 18/5/71, Lakewood, USA
Signed: US Soccer Federation,
1997
League Debut: 28/2/98

Steve Harkness
DOB: 27/8/71, Carlisle
Signed: Carlisle United, (£75,000)
July 1989
League Debut: 27/8/91

Paul Ince
DOB: 21/10/67, Ilford
Signed: Inter Milan, (£4.2 million)
July 1997
League Debut: 9/8/97

David James
DOB: 1/8/70, Welwyn Garden City
Signed: Watford, (£1 million)
July 1992
League Debut: 16/8/92

Bjorn Tore Kvarme
DOB: 17/7/72, Trondheim,
Norway
Signed: Rosenborg, January 1997
League Debut: 18/1/97

Oyvind Leonhardsen
DOB: 17/8/70, Norway
Signed: Wimbledon,
(£3.75 million) June 1997
League Debut: 18/10/97

Dominic Matteo
DOB: 24/4/74, Dumfries,
Scotland
Signed: Trainee, May 1992
League Debut: 23/10/93

Jason McAteer
DOB: 18/6/71, Birkenhead
Signed: Bolton Wanderers,
(£4.5 million) September 1995
League Debut: 16/9/95

Steve McManaman
DOB: 11//2/72, Bootle
Signed: Trainee, February 1990
League Debut: 15/12/90

Danny Murphy
DOB: 18/3/77, Chester
Signed: Crewe Alexandra,
(£1.5 million) July 1997
League Debut: 9/8/97

Michael Owen
DOB: 14/12/79, Chester
Signed: Trainee
League Debut: 6/5/97

Jamie Redknapp
DOB25/6/73, Barton on Sea
Signed: Bournemouth,
(£350,000) January 1991
League Debut: 7/12/91

Karlheinz Riedle
DOB: 16/9/65, Germany
Signed: Borussia Dortmund,
(£1.5 million) July 1997
League Debut: 9/8/97

Carl Serrant
DOB: 12/9/75, Bradford
Signed: Oldham Athletic,
(£1 million) May 1998
League Debut: TBA

1998-99 Premier League Fixtures

	Home	Away		Home	Away
Arsenal	22 Aug	9 Jan	Manchester United	6 Mar	26 Sep
Aston Villa	17 Apr	21 Nov	Middlesbrough	6 Feb	26 Dec
Blackburn Rovers	28 Nov	24 Apr	Newcastle United	28 Dec	29 Aug
Charlton Athletic	19 Sep	13 Feb	Nottingham Forest	24 Oct	5 Apr
Chelsea	3 Oct	27 Feb	Sheffield Wednesday	19 Dec	8 May
Coventry City	9 Sep	30 Jan	Southampton	16 Jan	15 Aug
Derby County	7 Nov	13 Mar	Tottenham Hotspur	1 May	5 Dec
Everton	3 Apr	17 Oct	West Ham United	20 Feb	12 Sep
Leeds United	14 Nov	10 Apr	Wimbledon	16 May	12 Dec
Leicester City	20 Mar	31 Oct			

Left: *Jamie Redknapp.* Mike Cooper/ Allsport

Transfers In: Sean Dundee (Karlsruhe £2m), Steve Staunton (Aston Villa free), Vegard Heggen (Rosenborg £3.5m)
Tranfers Out: Michael Thomas (Benfica free)

Below: Steve McManaman. Stu Forster/ Allsport

Liverpool

Chelsea

Above: *Player-manager Gianluca Vialli.* Stu Forster/Allsport

Right: *Gianfranco Zola.* Mark Thompson/Allsport

There's no doubt that, for the first time since the 1970s, Chelsea supporters viewed the 1997-98 season as the year the Blues would carry all before them. Inspired by dreadlocked Dutch player-manager and media darling Ruud Gullit, with a team of all-stars bought from top European clubs—Vialli, Petrescu, Leboeuf, di Matteo, Zola—and having broken their duck with the FA Cup victory in 1997, everything seemed set for the start of the 1997-98 season.

And they went off like a train. Brilliant victories against Barnsley (6–0), Wimbledon (2–0), Southampton (4–2) and Crystal Palace (3–2) put them into early season contention at the top of the Premiership and only a stunning 89th minute winner from Nigel Winterburn saw London rivals Arsenal win a fantastic five-goal match.

The trouble was that Chelsea could turn it on against the minnows, but they weren't resilient enough to take the draws elsewhere. 15 losses and 3 draws does not win a Premiership—in spite of a fantastic 71-goal haul (only bettered by Man U) and 20 wins. Something had to change, and for many supporters it seemed as if the sky had fallen in when dreadlocked Ruud Gullit was sacked, and Gianluca Vialli accepted his first position in management.

The choice, however, turned out to be inspired. A 3–1 victory over Arsenal in the second leg of the Coca-Cola Cup semi-final set up a final against Middlesbrough, the side they had beaten in 1997's FA Cup. The meeting on 29 March went to extra time but was, in the end, comfortably converted into a 2–0 victory for the Blues. On 13 May, in Stockholm, a Zola strike in the 71st minute against Stuttgart brought European silverware—the Cup Winners' Cup—to Stamford Bridge. These trophies have helped tempt more famous summer signings: French hard man Desailly, Albert Ferrer from Barcelona and the scintillating Brian Laudrup from Rangers.

Chelsea have spent much of their time in football's top drawer. Under Dave Sexton, the 1960s and beginning of the 1970s proved to be the club's most successful period. Three major trophies went to Stamford Bridge during these exciting years of Osgood, Hutchinson, Cooke and Bonetti, but since then, the club's fortunes have been mixed. For its legions of fans and for its controversial chairman Ken Bates, who has provided the financial muscle for first Glenn Hoddle, then Ruud Gullit and now Gianluca Vialli to build a side and a ground fit for the Premiership, 1998-99 must be payback time.

Season at a Glance

1997-98 Final Position: 4th in the Premiership
Top League Goalscorers: Flo: 12, Vialli: 11, Hughes: 9
Highest League win: 6-0 v Barnsley (A), 24 August 1997
Worst League Defeat: 2-4 v Liverpool (A), 5 October 1997
Highest Attendance: 34,845 v Bolton, 10 May 1998
Lowest Attendance: 29,075 v Sheffield Wed, 19 April 1998

PREMIER LEAGUE FOOTBALL

Chelsea

Managers

John Tait Robertson	1905-06
David Calderhead Snr	1907-33
Leslie Knighton	1933-39
Billy Birrell	1939-52
Ted Drake	1952-61
Tommy Docherty	1961-67
Dave Sexton	1967-74
Ron Suart	1974-75
Eddie McCreadie	1975-77
Ken Shellito	1977-78
Danny Blanchflower	1978-79
Geoff Hurst	1979-81
John Neal	1981-85
John Hollins	1985-88
Bobby Campbell	1988-91
Ian Porterfield	1991-93
David Webb	1993
Glenn Hoddle	1993-96
Ruud Gullit	1996-98
Gianluca Vialli	1998-

Above: *Player-manager Gianluca Vialli.*
Ross Kinnaird/Allsport

Right: *Tore Andre Flo.*
Ben Radford/Allsport

Honours

Division One Champions:	1954-55
Division Two Champions:	1983-84, 1988-89
Runners-up:	1906-07, 1911-12, 1929-30, 1962-63, 1976-77
FA Cup Winners:	1970, 1997
Runners-up:	1915, 1967, 1994
Football League Cup Winners:	1965, 1998
Runners-up:	1972
Full Members Cup Winners:	1986
Zenith Data Systems Cup Winners:	1990
Cup Winners' Cup Winners:	1971, 1998

Club Details

Year formed:	1905
Ground:	Stamford Bridge, London SW6 1HS
Nickname:	The Blues
Club Colours:	Blue and white
Manager:	Gianluca Vialli
Record attendance:	82,905 v Arsenal, 12 October 1935, Division One
Record League victory:	9-2 v Glossop North End, 1 September 1906, Division Two – Scorers: Hilsdon 5, Key, McDermott, Copeland, Kirwan
Record Cup victory:	13-0 v Jeunesse Hautcharage, 29 September 1971, European Cup Winners' Cup First Round second leg – Scorers: Osgood 5, Baldwin 3, Harris, Hollins (pen), Webb, Hudson, Houseman
Record defeat:	1-8 v Wolverhampton Wanderers, 26 September 1953, Division One
Highest League scorer in a season:	Jimmy Greaves, 41, 1960-61, Division One
Highest League scorer during career:	Bobby Tambling, 164, 1958-70
Most League appearances:	Ron Harris, 655, 1962-80

Chelsea

97/98 Results

August

3	Manchester United (CS)		L	1-1	M Hughes 52
		(Lost 4-2 on penalties)			
9	Coventry City	A	L	2-3	Sinclair 39, Flo 71
24	Barnsley	A	W	6-0	Petrescu 25, Poyet 38, Vialli 44, 57, 65, 82
27	Wimbledon	A	W	2-0	Di Matteo 60, Petrescu 64
30	Southampton	H	W	4-2	Petrescu 7, Leboeuf 28, Hughes 31, Wise 34

September

13	Crystal Palace	A	W	3-0	M Hughes 20, Leboeuf 26 (pen), Le Saux 90
18	Slovan Bratislava (ECWC 1-1)	H	W	2-0	Di Matteo 6, Granville 80
21	Arsenal	H	L	2-3	Poyet 40, Zola 60
24	Manchester United	A	D	2-2	Berg 25 (og), M Hughes 68
27	Newcastle United	H	W	1-0	Poyet 75

October

2	Slovan Bratislava (ECWC 1-2)	A	W	2-0	Vialli 27, Di Matteo 60
5	Liverpool	A	L	2-4	Zola 22, Poyet 85 (pen)
15	Blackburn Rovers (CCC 3)	H	W	1-1	Di Matteo 61
		(Won 4-1 on penalties)			

Frank Leboeuf.
Allsport

18	Leicester City	H	W	1-0	Leboeuf 88
23	Tromso (ECWC 2-1)	A	L	2-3	Vialli 85, 90
26	Bolton Wanderers	A	L	0-1	

November

1	Aston Villa	A	W	2-0	Hughes 38, Flo 82
6	Tromso (ECWC 2-2)	H	W	7-1	Petrescu 13, 86, Vialli 24, 61, 76, Zola 43, Leboeuf 55 (pen)
8	West Ham United	H	W	2-1	Ferdinand 57 (og), Zola 83
19	Southampton (CCC 4)	H	W	2-1	Flo 61, Morris 118
22	Blackburn Rovers	A	L	0-1	
26	Everton	H	W	2-0	Wise 80 (pen), Zola 90 (pen)
29	Derby County	H	W	4-0	Zola 12, 66, 77, Hughes 35

December

6	Tottenham Hotspur	A	W	6-1	Flo 40, 63, 90, Di Matteo 48, Petrescu 59, Nicholls 78
13	Leeds United	H	D	0-0	
20	Sheffield Wednesday	A	W	4-1	Petrescu 30, Vialli 56, Leboeuf 65 (pen), Flo 84
26	Wimbledon	H	D	1-1	Vialli 8
29	Southamton	A	L	0-1	

January

4	Manchester United (FAC 3)	H	L	3-5	Le Saux 78, Vialli 83, 88
7	Ipswich Town (CCC QF)	A	W	2-2	Flo 32, Le Saux 45 Won 4-1 on penalties
10	Coventry City	H	W	3-1	Nicholls 65, 70, Di Matteo 78
18	Everton	A	L	1-3	Flo 37
28	Arsenal (CCC SF-1)	A	L	1-2	Hughes 68
31	Barnsley	H	W	2-0	Vialli 23, Hughes 47

February

8	Arsenal	A	L	0-2	
18	Arsenal (CCC SF-2)	H	W	3-1	Hughes 10, Di Matteo 51, Petrescu 53
21	Leicester City	A	L	0-2	
28	Manchester United	H	L	0-1	

March

5	Real Betis (ECWC QF-1)	A	W	2-1	Flo 9, 12
8	Aston Villa	H	L	0-1	
11	Crystal Palace	H	W	6-2	Vialli 15, 44, Zola 17, Wise 84, Flo 89, 90
14	West Ham United	A	L	1-2	Charvet 54
19	Real Betis (ECWC QF-2)	H	W	3-1	Sinclair 30, Di Matteo 50, Zola 90
29	Middlesbrough (CCC F)		W	2-0	Sinclair 95, Di Matteo 107

April

2	Vicenza (ECWC SF-1)	A	L	0-1	
5	Derby County	A	W	1-0	M Hughes 37
8	Leeds United	A	L	1-3	Charvet 11
11	Tottenham Hotspur	H	W	2-0	Flo 75, Vialli 88
16	Vicenza (ECWC SF-2)	H	W	3-1	Poyet 35, Zola 51, Hughes 76
19	Sheffield Wednesday	H	W	1-0	Leboeuf 23 (pen)
25	Liverpool	H	W	4-1	Hughes 11, 78, Clarke 67, Flo 72
29	Blackburn Rovers	H	L	0-1	

May

2	Newcastle United	A	L	1-3	Di Matteo 77
10	Bolton Wanderers	H	W	2-0	Vialli 73, Morris 90
13	VfB Stuttgart (ECWC F)		W	1-0	Zola 71

Marcel Desailly.
Ben Radford/Allsport

PREMIER LEAGUE FOOTBALL

Chelsea

Squad

GOALKEEPERS
ED DE GOEY
KEVIN HITCHCOCK

DEFENDERS
ALBERT FERRER FRANK LEBEOUF MARCEL DESAILLY GRAEME LE SAUX
FRANK SINCLAIR STEVE CLARKE ANDY MYERS CELESTINE BABAYARO
MICHAEL DUBERRY

MIDFIELDERS
DAN PETRESCU ROBERTO DI MATTEO BERNARD LAMBOURDE GUSTAVO POYET
EDDIE NEWTON DENNIS WISE JODY MORRIS
BRIAN LAUDRUP

STRIKERS
PIERLUIGI CASIRAGHI TORE ANDRE FLO GIANLUCA VIALLI

GIANFRANCO ZOLA

Celestine Babayaro
DOB: 29/8/78, Kaduna, Nigeria
Signed: Anderlecht, (£2.5 million)
June 1997
League Debut: 18/10/97

Pierluigi Casiraghi
DOB: 4/3/69, Monza, Italy
Signed: Lazio, (£4.5 million) May
1998
League Debut: TBA

Steve Clarke
DOB: 29/8/63, Saltcoats, Scotland
Signed: St Mirren, (£422,000)
January 1987
League Debut: 24/1/87

Ed De Goey
DOB: 20/12/66, Gouda, Holland
Signed: Feyenoord, (£2.25 million)
June 1997
League Debut: 9/8/97

Marcel Desailly
DOB: 7/9/68, Ghana
Signed: AC Milan, (£5 million)
May 1998
League Debut: TBA

Roberto Di Matteo
DOB: 29/5/70, S'hausen,
Switzerland
Signed: Lazio, (£4.9 million)
July 1996
League Debut: 18/8/96

Albert Ferrer
DOB: 6/6/70, Barcelona, Spain
Signed: Barcelona, (£2.2 million)
June 1998
League Debut: TBA

Tore Andre Flo
DOB: 15/6/73, Stryn, Norway
Signed: FK Brann, (free)
June 1997
League Debut: 9/8/97

Kevin Hitchcock
DOB: 5/10/62, London
Signed: Mansfield Town,
(£250,000) March 1988
League Debut: 26/3/88

Bernard Lambourde
DOB: 11/5/71, Les Abysses,
France
Signed: Bordeaux, (£1.5 million)
June 1997
League Debut: 24/9/98

Graeme Le Saux
DOB: 17/10/68, Harrow
Signed: St Paul's Jersey, (free)
December 1987
League Debut: 13/5/89

Frank Leboeuf
DOB: 22/1/68, Marseilles, France
Signed: Strasbourg, (£2.5 million)
June 1996
League Debut: 18/8/96

Jody Morris
DOB: 22/12/68, London
Signed: Trainee, January 1996
League Debut: 4/2/96

Eddie Newton
DOB: 13/12/71, London
Signed: Trainee, May 1990
League Debut: 2/5/92

Dan Petrescu
DOB: 22/12/67, Bucharest,
Romania
Signed: Sheffield Wednesday,
(£2.3 million) November 1995
League Debut: 18/11/95

Gustavo Poyet
DOB: 15/11/67, Montevideo,
Uruguay
Signed: Real Zaragoza, (free)
June 1997
League Debut: 9/8/97

Frank Sinclair
DOB: 3/12/91, London
Signed: Trainee, May 1990
League Debut: 6/4/91

Gianluca Vialli
DOB: 9/7/64, Cremona, Italy
Signed: Sampdoria, (free)
May 1996
League Debut: 18/8/96

Dennis Wise
DOB: 15/12/66, London
Signed: Wimbledon,
(£1.6 million) July 1990
League Debut: 25/8/90

Gianfranco Zola
DOB: 5/7/66, Oliena, Italy
Signed: Parma, (£4.5 million)
November 1996
League Debut: 16/11/96

1998-99 Premier League Fixtures

	Home	Away		Home	Away
Arsenal	9 Sep	30 Jan	Manchester United	28 Dec	23 Sep
Aston Villa	31 Oct	20 Mar	Middlesbrough	26 Sep	6 Mar
Blackburn Rovers	13 Feb	19 Sep	Newcastle United	22 Aug	9 Jan
Charlton Athletic	17 Oct	3 Apr	Nottingham Forest	12 Sep	20 Feb
Coventry City	16 Jan	15 Aug	Sheffield Wednesday	28 Nov	24 Apr
Derby County	16 May	12 Dec	Southampton	6 Feb	26 Dec
Everton	1 May	5 Dec	Tottenham Hotspur	19 Dec	8 May
Leeds United	5 Apr	24 Oct	West Ham United	13 Mar	7 Nov
Leicester City	17 Apr	21 Nov	Wimbledon	14 Nov	10 Apr
Liverpool	27 Feb	3 Oct			

Transfers In: Pierluigi Casiraghi (Lazio £5.4m), Brian Laudrup (Rangers free), Marcel Desailly (AC Milan £4.6m), Albert Ferrer (Barcelona £2.2m)
Tranfers Out: Mark Hughes (Southampton £650,000), Danny Granville (Leeds £1.5m), Mark Stein (Bournemouth free)

Left: *Brian Laudrup.*
Clive Brunskill/Allsport

Below: *Stamford Bridge, home of Chelsea.*
Allsport

PREMIER LEAGUE FOOTBALL

Chelsea

Leeds Utd

Above: *Nigel Martyn.*
Alex Livesey/Allsport

Right: *Jimmy Hasselbaink.*
Michael Cooper/Allsport

Sustained success for Leeds' fans who can remember the string of triumphs during the Revie era has been a long time coming. In spite of a stable of good players, and a brilliant Cantona-orchestrated Division 1 triumph in 1991-92, the last years under Howard Wilkinson promised but did not deliver. Leeds needed a change and they got it in 1996 when George Graham took over. In his usual quiet way, he put together a team for the 1997-98 season that had an outside chance of big success. Certainly the firepower of Jimmy Floyd Hasselbaink, Rod Wallace, Alf Inge Haaland and Lee Sharpe gave them the cutting edge they needed for honours.

The start of the season proved otherwise: a plucky 1–1 draw away to Arsenal and a good 3–1 home victory over Sheffield Wednesday was followed by defeats against Palace, Liverpool and Villa. The opening match of September, a scintillating 4–3 victory over Blackburn Rovers, showed the qualities of the team—they could score goals, in this case four between the 3rd and 23rd minutes, but they could also let them in. An end of season a record of 57 for and 46 against was disappointing on both counts. Other than Hasselbaink (17) and Wallace (10), no one reached double figures and the defence was very un-George Graham. Defeats by Bristol City (1–2 in the Coca-Cola) and Reading (2–3 in the same competition) could have led other managers to feel concerned about their position, but good home form at the end of the season saved the day. Fifth place, and a coveted spot in Europe, gives plenty to look forward to in 1998-99.

Leeds United joined the Second Division in 1920 and enjoyed a respectable if undistinguished League career until the appointment of Don Revie as player-manager in 1961. He carefully fashioned a winning side from players developed in Leeds' youth scheme, although their style of play did little to endear them to the public. Success in both domestic and European competition continued, and with it came grudging respect.

Revie's departure for the England manager's job marked the beginning of a drop in standards. A succession of managers was unable to prevent a slow decline which included relegation to Division Two in 1982. Howard Wilkinson worked hard to rebuild the side, and his work has been continued by his successor. Both George Graham and Leeds United are used to success: it cannot be far away now.

Season at a Glance

1997-98 Final Position:	5th in the Premiership
Top League Goalscorers:	Hasselbaink: 17, Wallace: 10, Haaland: 7
Highest League win:	5-0 v Derby County (A), 15 March 1998
Worst League Defeat:	0-3 v West Ham United (A), 30 March 1998
	0-3 v Man United (A), 4 May 1998
Highest Attendance:	39,952 v Man United, 27 September 1997
Lowest Attendance:	28,791 v Southampton, 28 February 1998

PREMIER LEAGUE FOOTBALL

Leeds Utd

Managers

Above: *Manager George Graham.*
Ross Kinnaird/Allsport

Right: *Rod Wallace, who moved to Glasgow Rangers in the closed season.*
Ross Kinnaird/Allsport

Gilbert Gillies	1905-08
Frank Scott Walford	1908-12
Herbert Chapman	1912-19
Arthur Fairclough	1920-27
Dick Ray	1927-35
Billy Hampson	1935-47
Willis Edwards	1947-48
Frank Buckley	1948-53
Raich Carter	1953-58
Bill Lambton	1958-59
Jack Taylor	1959-61
Don Revie	1961-74
Brian Clough	1974
Jimmy Armfield	1974-78
Jock Stein	1978
Jimmy Adamson	1978-80
Allan Clarke	1980-82
Eddie Gray	1982-85
Billy Bremner	1985-88
Howard Wilkinson	1988-96
George Graham	1996-

Honours

Division One Champions:	1968-69, 1973-74, 1991-92
Runners-up:	1964-65, 1965-66, 1969-70, 1970-71, 1971-72
FA Cup Winners:	1972
Runners-up:	1965, 1970, 1973
Football League Cup Winners:	1968
European Cup Runners-up:	1975
European Cup Winners' Cup Runners-up:	1973
UEFA Cup Winners:	1973, 1976
European Fairs Cup Winners:	1968, 1971
Runners-up:	1967

Club Details

Year formed: 1919
Ground: Elland Road, Leeds LS11 0ES
Nickname: United
Club Colours: White
Manager: George Graham
Record attendance: 57,892 v Sunderland, 15 March 1967,
                                        FA Cup Fifth Round replay

Record League victory: 8-0 v Leicester City, 7 April 1934,
                                        Division One – Scorers: Mahon 2,
                                        Firth 2, Duggan 2, Furness 2

Record Cup victory: 10-0 v Lyn, 17 September 1969, European
                                        Cup First Round first leg – Scorers:
                                        Jones 3, Bremner 2, Clarke 2, Giles 2,
                                        O'Grady
Record defeat: 1-8 v Stoke City, 27 August 1934,
                                        Division One

Highest League scorer in a season: John Charles, 42, 1953-54, Division Two
Highest League scorer during career: Peter Lorimer, 168, 1969-75 and
                                        1983-86
Most League appearances: Jack Charlton, 629, 1953-73

97/98 Results

August

9	Arsenal	H	D	1-1	Hasselbaink 42
13	Sheffield Wednesday	A	W	3-1	Wallace 7, 62, Ribeiro 36
23	Crystal Palace	H	L	0-2	
26	Liverpool	H	L	0-2	
30	Aston Villa	A	L	0-1	

September

14	Blackburn Rovers	A	W	4-3	Wallace 3, 17, Molenaar 6, Hopkin 23
17	Bristol City (CCC 2-1)	H	W	3-1	Wetherall 20, Hasselbaink 70 (pen), Ribeiro 90
20	Leicester City	H	L	0-1	
24	Southampton	A	W	2-0	Molenaar 36, Wallace 55
27	Manchester United	H	W	1-0	Wetherall 34
30	Bristol City (CCC 2-2)	A	L	1-2	Hasselbaink 8

October

4	Coventry City	A	D	0-0	
15	Stoke City (CCC 3)	A	W	3-1	Kewell 69, Wallace 93, 105
18	Newcastle United	H	W	4-1	Ribeiro 30, Kewell 38, Beresford 43 og, Wetherall 47
25	Wimbledon	A	L	0-1	

Harry Kewell.
Shaun Botterill/Allsport

November

1	Tottenham Hotspur	A	W	1-0	Wallace 20
8	Derby County	H	W	4-3	Wallace 37, Kewell 40, Hasselbaink 82 (pen), Bowyer 90
18	Reading (CCC 4)	H	L	2-3	Wetherall 16, Bowyer 54
23	West Ham United	H	W	3-1	Hasselbaink 76, 90, Haaland 88
29	Barnsley	A	W	3-2	Haaland 35, Wallace 79, Lilley 82

December

6	Everton	H	D	0-0	
13	Chelsea	A	D	0-0	
20	Bolton Wanderers	H	W	2-0	Ribeiro 68, Hasselbaink 81
26	Liverpool	A	L	1-3	Haaland 84
28	Aston Villa	H	D	1-1	Hasselbaink 79

January

3	Oxford United (FAC 3)	H	W	4-0	Radebe 17, Hasselbaink 45 (pen) Kewell 71, 72
10	Arsenal	A	L	1-2	Hasselbaink 69
17	Sheffield Wednesday	H	L	1-2	Pembridge 63 og
24	Grimsby Town (FAC 4)	H	W	2-0	Molenaar 45, Hasselbaink 79
31	Crystal Palace	A	D	2-0	Wallace 7, Hasselbaink 13

February

7	Leicester City	A	L	0-1	
14	Birmingham City (FAC 5)	H	W	3-2	Wallace 5, Hasselbaink 28, 87
22	Newcastle United	A	D	1-1	Wallace 82
28	Southampton	H	L	0-1	

March

4	Tottenham Hotspur	H	W	1-0	Kewell 45
7	Wolves (FAC 6)	H	L	0-1	
11	Blackburn Rovers	H	W	4-0	Bowyer 48, Hasselbaink 53, Haaland 56, 89
15	Derby County	A	W	5-0	Laursen 8 og, Halle 36, Bowyer 42, Kewell 59, Hasselbaink 72
30	West Ham United	A	L	0-3	

April

4	Barnsley	H	W	2-1	Hasselbaink 20, Moses 80 og
8	Chelsea	H	W	3-1	Hasselbaink 7, 47, Wetherall 22
11	Everton	A	L	0-2	
18	Bolton Wanderers	A	W	3-2	Haaland 16, Halle 34, Hasselbaink 85
25	Coventry City	H	D	3-3	Hasselbaink 16, 28, Kewell 75

May

| 4 | Manchester United | A | L | 0-3 | |
| 10 | Wimbledon | H | D | 1-1 | Haaland 81 |

Alf Inge Haaland.
Phil Cole/Allsport

PREMIER LEAGUE FOOTBALL

Squad

GOALKEEPERS
NIGEL MARTYN
MARK BEENEY

DEFENDERS
GARY KELLY   GUNNAR HALLE   ROBERT MOLENAAR   IAN HARTE
MARK JACKSON   LUCAS RADEBE   DANNY GRANVILLE
DAVID ROBERTSON   DAVID WETHERALL

MIDFIELDERS
ALF INGE HAALAND   LEE BOWYER   ANDY GRAY   MARTIN HIDEN

DAVID HOPKIN   LEE SHARPE   BRUNO RIBEIRO

STRIKERS
JIMMY FLOYD HASSELBAINK
HARRY KEWELL   DEREK LILLEY   CLYDE WIJNHARD

Mark Beeney
DOB: 30/12/67, Pembury
Signed: Brighton, (£350,000)
April 1993
League Debut: 8/5/93

Lee Bowyer
DOB: 3/1/77, London
Signed: Charlton, (£2.6 million)
July 1996
League Debut: 17/8/96

Danny Granville
DOB: 19/1/75, London
Signed: Chelsea, (£1.5 million)
June 1998
League Debut: TBA

Andy Gray
DOB: 15/11/77, Harrogate, Yorks
Signed: Apprentice, July 1995
League Debut: 13/1/96

Alf Inge Haaland
DOB: 23/11/72, Stavanger,
Norway
Signed: Nottingham Forest,
(£1.6 million) June 1997
League Debut: 9/8/97

Gunnar Halle
DOB: 11/8/69, Oslo, Norway
Signed: Oldham Athletic,
(£400,000) December 1996
League Debut: 14/12/96

Ian Harte
DOB: 31/8/77, Drogheda, Eire
Signed: Apprentice, December
1995
League Debut: 13/1/96

Jimmy Floyd Hasselbaink
DOB: 27/3/72, Surinam
Signed: Boavista, (£2 million)
June 1997
League Debut: 9/8/97

Martin Hiden
DOB: 11/3/73, Stainz, Austria
Signed: Rapid Vienna,
(£1.5 million) February 1998
League Debut: 28/2/98

Mark Jackson
DOB: 30/9/77, Barnsley
Signed: Trainee, July 1995
League Debut: 30/3/96

David Hopkin
DOB: 21/8/70, Greenock,
Scotland
Signed: Crystal Palace,
(£3.25 million) July 1997
League Debut: 9/8/9

Gary Kelly
DOB: 9/7/74, Drogheda, Eire
Signed: Home Farm, (free) July
1991
League Debut: 22/12/91

Harry Kewell
DOB: 22/9/78, Sydney,
Australia
Signed: Australian Soccer
Academy, (free) July 1995
League Debut: 14/12/96

Derek Lilley
DOB: 9/2/74, Paisley, Scotland
Signed: Greenock Morton,
(£500,000) March 1997
League Debut: 7/4/97

Nigel Martyn
DOB: 11/8/66, St Austell,
Cornwall
Signed: Crystal Palace, (£2.25
million) July 1996
League Debut: 17/8/96

Robert Molenaar
DOB: 27/2/69, Holland
Signed: Volendam, January
1997
League Debut: 11/1/97

Lucas Radebe
DOB: 12/4/69, Johannesburg,
South Africa
Signed: Kaiser Chiefs,
(£250,000) September 1994
League Debut: 26/9/94

Bruno Ribeiro
DOB: 22/10/75, Setubal,
Portugal
Signed: Setubal, (£500,000),
July 1997
League Debut: 9/8/97

David Robertson
DOB: 17/10/68, Aberdeen,
Scotland
Signed: Glasgow Rangers,
(£500,000) June 1997
League Debut: 9/8/97

Lee Sharpe
DOB: 27/5/71, Halesowen
Signed: Manchester United,
(£4.5 million) August 1996
League Debut: 17/8/96

David Wetherall
DOB: 14/3/71, Sheffield
Signed: Sheffield Wednesday,
(£125,000) July 1991
League Debut: 3/9/91

Clyde Wijnhard
DOB: Unknown, Holland
Signed: Team, (£1.5 million)
June 1998
League Debut: TBC

1998-99 Premier League Fixtures

	Home	Away		Home	Away
Arsenal	8 May	19 Dec	Manchester United	24 Apr	28 Nov
Aston Villa	19 Sep	13 Feb	Middlesbrough	16 Jan	15 Aug
Blackburn Rovers	22 Aug	9 Jan	Newcastle United	6 Feb	26 Dec
Charlton Athletic	21 Nov	17 Apr	Nottingham Forest	3 Apr	17 Oct
Chelsea	24 Oct	5 Apr	Sheffield Wednesday	7 Nov	13 Mar
Coventry City	12 Dec	16 May	Southampton	8 Sep	30 Jan
Derby County	20 Mar	31 Oct	Tottenham Hotspur	6 Mar	26 Sep
Everton	20 Feb	12 Sep	West Ham United	5 Dec	1 May
Leicester City	3 Oct	27 Feb	Wimbledon	28 Dec	29 Aug
Liverpool	10 Apr	14 Nov			

Left: *Danny Granville, recent acquisition from Chelsea.*
l. Griffiths/Allsport

Below: *Elland Road, home of Leeds United.*
Graham Chadwick/Allsport

Transfers In: Clyde Wijnhard (Tiburg £1.5m), Danny Granville (Chelsea £1.5m)
Tranfers Out: Rod Wallace (Rangers free)

PREMIER LEAGUE FOOTBALL

Blackburn Rovers

Above: *Tim Flowers.*
Shaun Botterill/Allsport

Right: *Chris Sutton.*
Mike Hewitt/Allsport

For most teams under a recently-arrived manager, sixth place in the Premiership, including end of season victories over Chelsea and Newcastle, would have been considered success. But for a club that was runner-up in 1993-94, winner in 1994-95 and, at Christmas 1997, was strongly in contention again, it all felt a bit of a let down despite the prospect of Europe in 1998-99.

What a shame 1998 couldn't have continued like 1997. Revitalised by the shrewd talents of manager Roy Hodgson, ex-Inter Milan and Swiss National team supremo who took over from Ray Harford, the team certainly started well. Eleven Premiership wins—including a splendid 3–1 away win at Highbury and 1–0 at home to Chelsea—six draws and only two losses (3–4 away to Leeds and 0–4 to the in-form Manchester United) had put them firmly in contention. But seven losses in the Premiership run-in put paid to any title hopes and the change-round in form was shown graphically by the 4–1 caning at home administered by Champions-elect Arsenal.

In the end it was the defence that caused the problems—52 goals against, the 12th worst record in the Premiership—and the lack of goals from midfield: other than Sutton (18) and Gallacher (15), Tim Sherwood was next highest goalscorer with five. If Hodgson can put that right—and there's every likelihood with new signings Kevin Davies and Sebastien Perez that he will—then Blackburn will be vying for silverware once more.

Certainly the Ewood Park faithful have been used to waiting. Until the arrival of millionaire businessman Jack Walker, Blackburn Rovers was a museum piece, typical of the Lancashire clubs which had dominated the Football League (they were founder members) but had seen players and supporters slip away to more fashionable rivals.

Walker's input changed all that. Former Liverpool manager Kenny Dalglish was persuaded to cut short his retirement in October 1991, and his recruitment attracted international players of the calibre of England regulars Tim Flowers, Graeme Le Saux and, most notably, striker Alan Shearer. The Ewood Park ground, home since 1890, was rebuilt and Premier League silverware followed shortly.

Then the bombshell: Shearer left for Newcastle; so, later, did Batty and, ultimately, Dalglish too. Ray Harford took over, and did much to retain Blackburn in the top flight during these difficult times. But Rovers' return to the top flight under Dalglish had ended a 26-year exile: no one wanted to see the renaissance halted and the stage was set for Hodgson.

Season at a Glance

1997-98 Final Position:	6th, Premiership
Top League Goalscorers:	Sutton: 18, Gallacher: 16, Sherwood: 5
Highest League win:	7-2 v Sheffield Wednesday (H), 25 August 1997
Worst League Defeat:	0-4 v Man United (A), 30 November1997
	0-4 v Leeds United (A), 11 March 1998
Highest Attendance:	30,547 v Man United, 6 April 1998
Lowest Attendance:	19,086 v Coventry City, 28 September

PREMIER LEAGUE FOOTBALL

Blackburn Rovers

Managers

Jack Carr	1922-26
Bob Crompton	1926-31
Arthur Barritt	1931-36
Reg Taylor	1936-38
Bob Crompton	1938-41
Eddie Hapgood	1946-47
Will Scott	1947
Jack Bruton	1947-49
Jackie Bestall	1949-53
Johnny Carey	1953-58
Dally Duncan	1958-60
Jack Marshall	1960-67
Eddie Quigley	1967-70
John Carey	1970-71
Ken Furphy	1971-73
Gordon Lee	1974-75
Jim Smith	1975-78
Jim Iley	1978
John Pickering	1978-79
Howard Kendall	1979-81
Bobby Saxton	1981-86
Don Mackay	1987-91
Kenny Dalglish	1991-95
Ray Harford	1995-96
Roy Hodgson	1997-

Above: *Roy Hodgson.*
Phil Cole/Allsport

Right: *Colin Hendry,*
who stunned Blackburn
fans by moving to Rangers
in August 1998.
Ross Kinnaird/Allsport

Honours

Premier League Champions:	1994-95
Runners-up:	1993-94
Division One Champions:	1911-12, 1913-14
Division Two Champions:	1938-39
Runners-up:	1957-58
Division Three Champions:	1974-75
Runners-up:	1979-80
FA Cup Winners:	1884, 1885, 1886, 1890, 1891, 1928
Runners-up:	1882, 1960
Football League Cup Winners:	1965, 1998
Runners-up:	1972
Full Members Cup Winners:	1987

Club Details

Year formed:	1875
Ground:	Ewood Park, Blackburn BB2 4JF
Nickname:	Rovers
Club Colours:	Blue and white
Manager:	Roy Hodgson
Record attendance:	61,783 v Bolton Wanderers, 2 March 1929, FA Cup Sixth Round
Record League victory:	9-2 v Glossop North End, 1 September 1906, Division Two – Scorers: Hilsdon 5, Key, McDermott, Copeland, Kirwan
Record Cup victory:	9-0 v Middlesbrough, 6 November 1954, Division Two – Scorers: Mooney 3, Quigley 3, Crossan 2, Langton
Record defeat:	0-8 v Arsenal, 25 February 1933, DivisionOne
Highest League scorer in a season:	Ted Harper, 43, 1925-26, Division One
Highest League scorer during career:	Simon Garner, 168, 1978-92
Most League appearances:	Derek Fazackerley, 596, 1970-86

Blackburn Rovers

97/98 Results

August

9	Derby County	H	W	1-0	Gallacher 20
13	Aston Villa	A	W	4-0	Sutton 21, 25, 41, Gallacher 71
23	Liverpool	H	D	1-1	Dahlin 84
25	Sheffield Wednesday	H	W	7-2	Gallacher 3, 7, Hyde 10 og, Wilcox 20, Sutton 24, 74
30	Crystal Palace	A	W	2-1	Sutton 23, Gallacher 31

September

14	Leeds United	H	L	3-4	Gallacher 8, Sutton 16 (pen), Dahlin 33
17	Preston North End (CCC 2-1)	H	W	6-0	Dahlin 26, 54, Sutton 29, Gallacher 78, Andersson 84, Bohinen 89
20	Tottenham Hotspur	A	D	0-0	
24	Leicester City	A	D	1-1	Sutton 36
28	Coventry City	H	D	0-0	
30	Preston North End (CCC 2-2)	A	L	0-1	

Kevin Davies while playing for Southampton.
Phil Cole/Allsport

October

4	Wimbledon	A	W	1-0	Sutton 6
15	Chelsea (CCC 3)	A	L	1-1	McKinlay 47 (Lost 4-1 on penalties)
18	Southampton	H	W	1-0	Sherwood 26
25	Newcastle	A	D	1-1	Sutton 57

November

1	Barnsley	A	D	1-1	Sherwood 30
8	Everton	H	W	3-2	Gallacher 37, Duff 81, Sherwood 84
22	Chelsea	H	W	1-0	Croft 11
30	Man Utd	A	L	0-4	

December

1	Bolton	H	W	3-1	Gallacher 4, Sutton 21, Wilcox 90
13	Arsenal	A	W	3-1	Wilcox 57, Gallacher 65, Sherwood 89
20	West Ham	H	W	3-0	Ripley 22, Duff 51, 72
26	Shef Wed	A	D	0-0	
28	Crystal Palace	H	D	2-2	Gallacher 27, Sutton 78

January

3	Wigan Athletic (FAC 3)	H	W	4-2	McGibbon 20 og, Gallacher 37, 60, Sherwood 48
11	Derby County	A	L	1-3	Sutton 87
17	Aston Villa	H	W	5-0	Sherwood 21, Gallacher 29, 54, 68, Ripley 81
26	Sheffield Wed'day (FAC 4)	A	W	3-0	Sutton 6, Sherwood 37, Duff 87
31	Liverpool	A	D	0-0	

February

7	Tottenham Hotspur	H	L	0-3	
14	West Ham United (FAC 5)	A	D	2-2	Gallacher 3, Sutton 62
21	Southampton	A	L	0-3	
25	West Ham (FAC 5R)	H	L	1-1	Ripley 115
	(Lost 4-5 on penalties)				
28	Leicester City	H	W	5-3	Dahlin 11, Sutton 25, 45, 47, Hendry 63

March

11	Leeds United	A	L	0-4	
14	Everton	A	L	0-1	
31	Barnsley	H	W	2-1	Dahlin 8, Gallacher 87

April

6	Man United	H	L	1-3	Sutton 32 (pen)
11	Bolton	A	L	1-2	Duff 51
13	Arsenal	H	L	1-4	Gallacher 51
18	West Ham	A	L	1-2	Wilcox 45
25	Wimbledon	H	D	0-0	
29	Chelsea	A	W	1-0	Gallacher 48

May

| 2 | Coventry City | A | L | 0-2 | |
| 10 | Newcastle | H | W | 1-0 | Sutton 88 |

Emile Henchoz.
Shaun Botterill/Allsport

PREMIER LEAGUE FOOTBALL

Blackburn Rovers

Squad

GOALKEEPERS
TIM FLOWERS
ALAN FETTIS
JOHN FILAN

DEFENDERS
JEFF KENNA   COLIN HENDRY   DARREN PEACOCK   GARY CROFT
STEPHANE HENCHOZ   PATRICK VALERY   TORE PEDERSEN

MIDFIELDERS
ANDERS ANDERSSON   GARY FLITCROFT   DAMIEN DUFF   SEBASTIAN PEREZ
TIM SHERWOOD   BILLY McKINLAY
JASON WILCOX   ADAM REED

STRIKERS
KEVIN DAVIES   MARTIN DAHLIN   KEVIN GALLACHER
CHRIS SUTTON   PER PEDERSEN
JIMMY CORBET

Anders Andersson
DOB: 15/3/74, Tomellia,
Switzerland
Signed: Malmo, (£500,000)
June 1997
League Debut: 9/8/97

Gary Croft
DOB: 17/2/74, Burton on Trent
Signed: Grimsby Town,
(£1.7 million) March 1996
League Debut: 28/9/96

Martin Dahlin
DOB:16/4/68, Uddevalla, Sweden
Signed: Roma, (£2 million) July
1997
League Debut: 9/8/97

Kevin Davies
DOB: 26/3/77, Sheffield
Signed: Southampton,
(£7.25 million) June 1998
League Debut: TBA

Damien Duff
DOB: 2/3/79, Ballyboden, Eire
Signed: Not known
League Debut: 11/5/97

Alan Fettis
DOB: 1/2/71, Belfast, N Ireland
Signed: Nottingham Forest, 1997
League Debut: 26/12/97

John Filan
DOB: 8/2/70, Sydney, Australia
Signed: Coventry City, (£500,000)
June 1997
League Debut: 9/8/97

Gary Flitcroft
DOB: 6/11/72, Bolton
Signed: Manchester City,
(£3.2 million) March 1996
League Debut: 30/3/96

Tim Flowers
DOB: 3/2/67, Kenilworth
Signed: Southampton,
(£2.4 million) November 1993
League Debut: 6/11/93

Kevin Gallacher
DOB: 23/11/66, Clydebank
Signed: Coventry City,
(£1.5 million) March 1993
League Debut: 3/4/93

Stephane Henchoz
DOB: 7/9/74, Switzerland
Signed: SV Hamburg,
(£2.5 million) June 1997
League Debut: 9/8/97

Colin Hendry
DOB: 7/12/65, Keith, Scotland
Signed: Dundee, (£30,000)
March 1987
League Debut: 14/3/87

Jeff Kenna
DOB: 27/8/70, Dublin, Eire)
Signed: Southampton,
(£1.5 million) March 1995
League Debut: 18/3/95

Billy McKinlay
DOB: 22/4/69, Glasgow
Signed: Dundee United,
(£1.75 million) October 1995
League Debut: 21/10/95

Darren Peacock
DOB: 3/2/68, Bristol
Signed: Newcastle United, (free)
June 1998
League Debut: TBA

Per Pedersen
DOB: 30/3/69, Aalborg,
Denmark
Signed: Odense
League Debut: 22/2/97

Tim Sherwood
DOB: 6/2/69, St Albans
Signed: Norwich City,
(£500,000) February 1992
League Debut: 22/2/92

Chris Sutton
DOB: 10/3/73, Nottingham
Signed: Norwich City,
(£5 million) July 1994
League Debut: 20/8/94

Patrick Valery
DOB: 3/7/69, Brignoles,
France
Signed: Bastia, (free)
June 1997
League Debut: 9/8/97

Jason Wilcox
DOB: 15/7/71, Farnworth
Signed: Trainee, June 1989
League Debut: 16/4/90

1998-99 Premier League Fixtures

	Home	Away		Home	Away
Arsenal	24 Oct	5 Apr	Manchester United	10 Apr	14 Nov
Aston Villa	26 Dec	6 Feb	Middlesbrough	3 Apr	17 Oct
Charlton Athletic	5 Dec	1 May	Newcastle United	12 Dec	16 May
Chelsea	19 Sep	13 Feb	Nottingham Forest	8 May	19 Dec
Coventry City	7 Nov	13 Mar	Sheffield Wednesday	20 Feb	12 Sep
Derby County	15 Aug	16 Jan	Southampton	21 Nov	17 Apr
Everton	6 Mar	26 Sep	Tottenham Hotspur	30 Jan	9 Sep
Leeds United	9 Jan	22 Aug	West Ham United	3 Oct	27 Feb
Leicester City	29 Aug	28 Dec	Wimbledon	20 Mar	31 Oct
Liverpool	24 Apr	28 Nov			

Transfers In: Kevin Davies (Southampton £7.5m), Sebastien Perez (Bastia £3m), Jim Corbett (Gillingham £1m), Darren Peacock (Newcastle free)
Tranfers Out: Stuart Ripley (Southampton £1.5m), James Beattie (Southampton free), Patrick Valery (Bastia £800,000), Colin Hendry (Glasgow Rangers £4m)

Left: *Damien Duff.*
Shaun Botterill/Allsport

Below: *Ewood Park, home of Blackburn.*
Shaun Botterill/Allsport

PREMIER LEAGUE FOOTBALL

Blackburn Rovers

Aston Villa

Above: *Lee Hendry.*
Stu Forest/Allsport

Right: *Stan Collymore.*
Allsport

Four straight losses at the start of the season to Leicester, Blackburn, Newcastle and Spurs effectively put paid to the Villans' title pretensions for another season and made Brian Little's security of tenure severely doubtful. Despite the seemingly good foundations for a strong Premiership contention—the excellent Bosnich in goal, Southgate and Ehiogu in defence, Collymore and Yorke in attack—the team was unable to put enough goals together to threaten. In total only 49 chances were converted—ranking the team 12th in the Premiership—and only Dwight Yorke got into double figures.

Four losses in five Premiership games at the end of January and in February, the disappointment of going out 0–1 to Coventry in the fifth round of the FA Cup, and the loss of manager Brian Little, confirmed that Villa was in freefall: was there a parachute or would they keep plummeting?

Reports of their demise were unfounded. Former player John Gregory, manager at lowly Wycombe, was the surprise choice to succeed Little, but he rose to the job admirably steering the club to European qualification by motivating the players. Certainly their abilities, when they expressed them on the pitch, were indisputable: the narrowest possible loss in the EUFA Cup Quarter-final—on an away goal—to Spanish Atletico Madrid showcased the talents that had been found wanting in the Premiership. Nine wins in 11 games at the end of the season, a better run-in than any other team, pushed them into seventh spot in the Premiership table and they had the satisafction of defeating three of the top four in this run: Liverpool, Chelsea and, their last game of the season, Champions Arsenal. If the Villans can come off the blocks showing that form in 1998-99, then anything's possible!

Birmingham's senior club by just one year, Aston Villa have always considered themselves a cut above their rivals, not only in terms of top-flight status but also because of the Villa Park ground, scene of many Cup semi-finals and in 1996 a European Championship venue.The trophy cabinet has also seen many trophies, with Villa just one behind Liverpool in terms of League Cup wins. Only Man U and Spurs have more FA Cup wins.

In modern times, the crowning achievement was the European Cup campaign of 1981-82, following on from their seventh Championship. It was a bizarre season, with manager Ron Saunders, in charge since 1974, resigning in February, leaving assistant Tony Barton to guide the team past Bayern Munich in Rotterdam by a single goal.

The mid-1990s team looked capable of further glory, combining proven internationals like Eire's Townsend with up and coming stars like England Under 21 defender Ugo Ehiogu but, as yet, it's been all promise and no substance.

Season at a Glance

1997-98 Final Position:	7th in the Premiership
Top League Goalscorers:	Yorke: 12, Joachim: 8, Milosevic: 7
Highest League win:	4-1 v Spurs (H), 26 December 1997
	4-1 v Everton (A), 28 March 1998
Worst League Defeat:	0-5 v Blackburn (A), 17 January 1998
Highest Attendance:	39,377 v Liverpool, 28 February 1998
Lowest Attendance:	29,343 v Southampton, 20 December 1997

Aston Villa

Managers

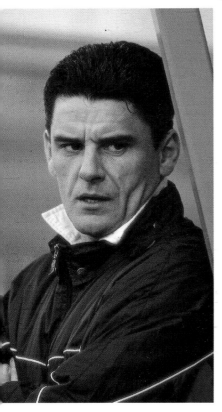

Jimmy McMullan	1934-36
Jimmy Hogan	1936-39
Alex Massie	1945-50
George Martin	1950-53
Eric Houghton	1953-58
Joe Mercer	1958-64
Dick Taylor	1964-67
Tommy Cummings	1967-68
Tommy Docherty	1968-70
Vic Crowe	1970-74
Ron Saunders	1974-82
Tony Barton	1982-84
Graham Turner	1984-86
Billy McNeill	1986-87
Graham Taylor	1987-90
Josef Venglos	1990-91
Ron Atkinson	1991-94
Brian Little	1994-98
John Gregory	1998-

Above: *John Gregory.*
Graham Chadwick/Allsport

Right: *Mark Bosnich.*
Michael Cooper/Allsport

Honours

Division One Champions:	1893-94, 1895-96, 1896-97 (Double), 1898-99, 1899-1900, 1909-10, 1980-81
Runners-up:	1888-89, 1902-03, 1907-08, 1910-11, 1912-13, 1913-14, 1930-31, 1932-33, 1989-90, 1992-93
Division Two Champions:	1937-38, 1959-60
Runners-up:	1974-75, 1987-88
FA Cup Winners:	1887, 1895, 1897 (Double), 1905, 1913, 1920, 1957
Runners-up:	1892, 1924
Football League Cup Winners:	1961, 1975, 1977, 1994, 1996
Runners-up:	1963, 1971
European Cup Winners:	1982
European Super Cup Winners:	1983

Club Details

Year formed:	1874
Ground:	Villa Park, Trinity Road, Birmingham B6 6HE
Nickname:	The Villans
Club Colours:	Claret and blue
Manager:	John Gregory
Record attendance:	76,588 v Derby County, 2 March 1946, FA Cup Sixth Round
Record League victory:	12-2 v Accrington Stanley, 12 March 1892, Division One – Scorers: Devey 4, Campbell 4, Dickson 2, Athersmith, Hodgetts
Record Cup victory:	13-0 v Wednesbury Old Athletic, 30 October 1886, FA Cup First Round – Scorers: Brown 3, Hunter 3, Burton 2, Loach 2, Hodgetts 2, Davis
Record defeat:	1-8 v Blackburn Rovers, 16 February 1889, FA Cup Third Round
Highest League scorer in a season:	'Pongo' Waring, 49, 1930-31, Division One
Highest League scorer during career:	Harry Hampton, 215, 1904-15
Most League appearances:	Charlie Aitken, 561, 1961-76

Aston Villa

97/98 Results

August

9	Leicester City	A	L	0-1	
13	Blackburn Rovers	H	L	0-4	
23	Newcastle United	A	L	0-1	
27	Tottenham Hotspur	A	L	2-3	Yorke 27, Collymore 58
30	Leeds United	H	W	1-0	Yorke 67

September

13	Barnsley	A	W	3-0	Ehiogu 25, Draper 50, Taylor 72
16	Bordeaux (UEFA 1-1)	A	D	0-0	
20	Derby County	H	W	2-1	Yorke 73, Joachim 75
22	Liverpool	A	L	0-3	
27	Sheffield Wednesday	H	W	2-0	Staunton 22, Taylor 49
30	Bordeaux (UEFA 1-2)	H	W	1-0	Milosevic 111

October

4	Bolton	A	W	1-0	Milosevic 12
15	West Ham (CCC 3)	A	L	0-3	
18	Wimbledon	H	L	1-2	Taylor 45
21	Atletico Bilbao (UEFA 2-1)	A	D	0-0	
26	Arsenal	A	D	0-0	

November

1	Chelsea	H	L	0-2	
4	Atletico Bilbao (UEFA 2-2)	H	W	2-1	Taylor 27, Yorke 50
8	Crystal Palace	A	D	1-1	Joachim 86
22	Everton	H	W	2-1	Milosevic 36, Ehiogu 56
25	Bucharest (UEFA 3-1)	A	L	1-2	Yorke 54
29	West Ham	A	L	1-2	Yorke 47

December

6	Coventry	H	W	3-0	Collymore 21, Hendrie 71, Joachim 85
9	Bucharest (UEFA 3-2)	H	W	2-0	Milosevic 71, Taylor 85
15	Man Utd	A	L	0-1	
20	Southampton	H	D	1-1	Taylor 64
26	Spurs	H	W	4-1	Draper 38, 68, Collymore 81, 89
28	Leeds United	A	D	1-1	Milosevic 85

Dwight Yorke.
Laurence Griffiths/Allsport

January

3	Portsmouth (FAC 3	A	D	2-2	Staunton 41, Grayson 88
10	Leicester City	H	D	1-1	Joachim 87
14	Portsmouth (FAC 3R)	H	W	1-0	Milosevic 21
17	Blackburn Rovers	A	L	0-5	
24	West Brom (FAC 4)	H	W	4-0	Grayson 4, Yorke 62, 64, Collymore 72

February

1	Newcastle United	H	L	0-1	
7	Derby County	A	W	1-0	Yorke 90
14	Coventry City (FAC 5)	H	L	0-1	
18	Manchester United	H	L	0-2	
21	Wimbledon	A	L	1-2	Milosevic 41
28	Liverpool	H	W	2-1	Collymore 10, 65

March

2	Atletico Madrid (UEFA QF-1)	A	L	0-1	
8	Chelsea	A	W	1-0	Joachim 51
11	Barnsley	H	L	0-1	
14	Crystal Palace	H	W	3-1	Taylor 1, Milosevic 15 (pen), 36
17	Atletico Madrid (UEFA QF-2)	H	W	2-1	Taylor 72, Collymore 74
28	Everton	A	W	4-1	Joachim 12, Charles 62, Yorke 72 (pen), 81

April

4	West Ham United	H	W	2-0	Joachim 77, Milosevic 83
11	Coventry City	A	W	2-1	Yorke 5, 48
18	Southampton	A	W	2-1	Hendrie 6, Yorke 60
25	Bolton Wanderers	H	L	1-3	Taylor 57

May

| 2 | Sheff Wed | A | W | 3-1 | Yorke 21, Hendrie 25, Joachim 50 |
| 10 | Arsenal | H | W | 1-0 | Yorke 37 (pen) |

Gareth Southgate.
Shaun Botterill/Allsport

PREMIER LEAGUE FOOTBALL

Aston Villa

Squad

GOALKEEPERS
MARK BOSNICH
MICHAEL OAKES

DEFENDERS
GARY CHARLES   UGO EHIOGU   GARETH SOUTHGATE   RICCARDO SCIMECA
SIMON GRAYSON   ALAN WRIGHT

MIDFIELDERS
GARETH BARRY   MARK DRAPER   IAN TAYLOR   ALAN THOMPSON
DARIUS VASSELL   FABIO FERRERASI   DAVID HUGHES

STRIKERS
DWIGHT YORKE   STAN COLLYMORE   LEE HENDRIE
JULIAN JOACHIM

Gareth Barry
DOB: 23/2/81, Hastings
Signed: Apprentice
League Debut: 2/5/98

Mark Bosnich
DOB: 13/1/72, Sydney, Australia
Signed: Sydney Croatia,
(free transfer) February 1992
League Debut: 25/4/92

Gary Charles
DOB: 13/4/70, London
Signed: Derby County,
(£2.9 million with Tommy
Johnson) January 1995
League Debut: 21/1/95

Fabio Ferrerasi
DOB: Not Known, Italy
Signed: Cesena, June 1998
League Debut: TBA

Stan Collymore
DOB:22/1/71, Stone
Signed: Liverpool, (£7 million)
May 1997
League Debut: 9/8/97

Mark Draper
DOB: 11/11/70, Nottingham
Signed: Leicester City,
(£3.25 million) July 1995
League Debut: 19/8/96

Ugo Ehiogu
DOB: 3/11/72, Hackney, London
Signed: West Bromwich Albion,
(£40,000) July 1991
League Debut: 24/8/91

Simon Grayson
DOB: 16/12/69, Ripon
Signed: Leicester City,
(£1.35 million) July 1997
League Debut: 13/8/97

Lee Hendrie
DOB: 18/577, Birmingham
Signed: Apprentice, May 1994
League Debut: 23/12/95

David Hughes
DOB: 1/2/78, Wrexham
Signed: Trainee
League Debut: 2/3/97

Julian Joachim
DOB: 20/9/74, Peterborough
Signed: Leicester City,
(£1.5 million) February 1996
League Debut: 24/2/96

Fernando Nelson
DOB: 5/11/71, Lisbon, Portugal
Signed: Sporting Lisbon,
(£1.75 million) July 1996
League Debut: 24/8/96

Michael Oakes
DOB: 30/10/73, Northwich,
Cheshire
Signed: Apprentice, July 1991
League Debut: 17/8/96

Riccardo Scimeca
DOB: 13/6/75, Leamington Spa
Signed: Apprentice, July 1993
League Debut: 19/8/95

Gareth Southgate
DOB: 3/9/70. Watford
Signed: Crystal Palace,
(£2.5 million) July 1995
League Debut: 19/8/95

Ian Taylor
DOB: 4/6/68, Birmingham
Signed: Port Vale, (£1 million)
December 1994
League Debut: 26/12/94

Alan Thompson
DOB: 22/12/73, Newcastle
Signed: Bolton, (£4.5 million)
June 1998
League Debut: TBA

Darius Vassell
DOB: 30/6/80, Birmingham
Signed: Trainee
League Debut: TBA

Alan Wright
DOB: 28/9/71, Ashton under
Lyme
Signed: Blackburn Rovers,
(£900,000) April 1995
League Debut: 18/3/95

Dwight Yorke
DOB: 3/11/71, Canaan, Tobago
Signed: St Clairs, (£120,000)
December 1989
League Debut: 17/3/90

1998-99 Premier League Fixtures

	Home	Away		Home	Away
Arsenal	12 Dec	16 May	Manchester United	5 Dec	1 May
Blackburn Rovers	6 Feb	26 Dec	Middlesbrough	22 Aug	9 Jan
Charlton Athletic	8 May	19 Dec	Newcastle United	9 Sep	30 Jan
Chelsea	20 Mar	31 Oct	Nottingham Forest	24 Apr	28 Nov
Coventry City	27 Feb	3 Oct	Sheffield Wednesday	28 Dec	29 Aug
Derby County	26 Sep	6 Mar	Southampton	10 Apr	14 Nov
Everton	16 Jan	15 Aug	Tottenham Hotspur	7 Nov	13 Mar
Leeds United	13 Feb	19 Sep	West Ham United	3 Apr	17 Oct
Leicester City	24 Oct	5 Apr	Wimbledon	12 Sep	20 Feb
Liverpool	21 Nov	17 Apr			

Transfers In: Alan Thompson (Bolton £4.5m), Fabrizio Ferrerasi (Cesena free), David Unsworth (West Ham Utd £3.m)
Tranfers Out: Savo Milosevic (Real Zaragoza £3.5m), Steve Staunton Liverpool free), Fernando Nelson (Porto £1.5m)

Above Left: *Alan Thompson in Bolton colours.*
Mark Thompson/Allsport

Left: *Julian Joachim.*
Ross Kinnaird/Allsport

Aston Villa

West Ham Utd

Above: *Trevor Sinclair.*
Mark Thompson/Allsport

Right: *Rio Ferdinand.*
Ben Radford/Allsport

West Ham United have always had a reputation as a skilful footballing team—and like many such outfits their honours board does not reflect the admiration in which they're held within the game. The 1997-98 season proved no exception to this rule.

They struggled initially under Harry Redknapp—their second consecutive former player to become manager—as a plethora of foreign imports failed to gel. But after flirting with relegation in 1996-97, '97-98 brought a surer touch, with John Hartson (a record buy from Arsenal) topping their list of goalscorers with 15, including two in the 2–1 home victory against Liverpool and one against Manchester United in a game West Ham were unlucky to lose 2–1; Trevor Sinclair (QPR's highly rated midfielder) and Israeli midfielder Eyal Berkovic were both outstanding in a mainly British-based team that only just missed out on Europe.

The West Ham year can be summed up in the five games it played against the season's success story, Arsenal. After an early season drubbing (4–0 at Highbury) and a 0–0 at Upton Park in the Premiership, the three cup games they played together were classics with West Ham going out to their London rivals in the quarter-finals of both FA and Coca-Cola Cups, the former 2–1 the latter unluckily 3–4 on penalties after a replay had ended tied at 1–1, as had the previous game. Just how close are success and failure at the top level!

Elected to Division Two in 1919, the Hammers' best spell in trophy terms came in the first five years of Ron Greenwood's reign: FA Cup Winners against Preston North End in 1964, they went on to take the European Cup Winners' Cup the following season. And while 1966 was a blank year club-wise, the trio of Geoff Hurst, Bobby Moore and Martin Peters were to make it a winning Wembley hat-trick by playing in England's victorious Jules Rimet Trophy campaign, Hurst scoring a hat-trick and Moore captaining the side.

Greenwood would go on to steer the national team's fortunes, but the club which has yet to win the League title found honours hard to come by. FA Cup wins over capital opposition in 1975 (over Fulham) and 1980 (Arsenal) remain their most recent trophies, in both cases gained under the managership of John Lyall. After a number of managers, fans' choice Billy Bonds (who took the club down and up again) left in 1994 amid mystery, which was when his assistant Harry Redknapp assumed command. He has put together the makings of a useful team that will be looking forward to the '98-99 season.

Season at a Glance

1997-98 Final Position:	8th in the Premiership
Top League Goalscorers:	Hartson: 15, Berkovic: 7, Sinclair: 7
Highest League win:	6-0 v Barnsley (H), 10 January 1998
Worst League Defeat:	0-5 v Liverpool (A), 2 May 1998
Highest Attendance:	25,908 v Liverpool, 27 September 1997
Lowest Attendance:	22,477 v Coventry City, 26 December 1997

PREMIER LEAGUE FOOTBALL

West Ham Utd

Managers

Syd King	1901-32
Charlie Paynter	1932-50
Ted Fenton	1950-61
Ron Greenwood	1961-74
John Lyall	1974-89
Lou Macari	1989-90
Billy Bonds	1990-94
Harry Redknapp	1994-

Above: *Harry Redknapp.*
Alex Livesey/Allsport

Right: *Eyal Berkovic.*
Mark Thompson/Allsport

Honours

Division One Runners-up:	1992-93
Division Two Champions:	1957-58, 1980-81
Runners-up:	1922-23, 1990-91
FA Cup Winners:	1964, 1975, 1980
Runners-up:	1923
Football League Cup Runners-up:	1966, 1981
European Cup Winners' Cup Winners:	1965
Runners-up:	1976

Club Details

Year formed:	1895
Ground:	Boleyn Ground, Green Street, Upton Park, London E13 9AZ
Nickname:	The Hammers
Club Colours:	Claret and white
Manager:	Harry Redknapp
Record attendance:	42,322 v Tottenham Hotspur, 17 October 1970, Division One
Record League victory:	8-0 v Rotherham United, 8 March 1958, Division Two – Scorers: Dick 4, Smith 2, Keeble 2; 8-0 v Sunderland, 19 October 1968, Division One – Scorers: Hurst 6, Moore, Brooking
Record Cup victory:	10-0 v Bury, 25 October 1983, League Cup Second Round second leg – Scorers: Cottee 4, Devonshire 2, Brooking 2, Stewart, Martin
Record defeat:	2-8 v Blackburn Rovers, 26 December 1963, Division One
Highest League scorer in a season:	Vic Watson, 41, 1929-30, Division One
Highest League scorer during career:	Vic Watson, 298, 1920-35
Most League appearances:	Billy Bonds, 663, 1967-88

West Ham Utd

97/98 Results

August

9	Barnsley	A	W	2-1	Hartson 53, Lampard 76
13	Tottenham Hotspur	H	W	2-1	Hartson 4, Berkovic 70
23	Everton	A	L	1-2	Watson 23 og
27	Coventry City	A	D	1-1	Kitson 64
30	Wimbledon	H	W	3-1	Hartson 48, Rieper 54, Berkovic 55

September

13	Manchester United	A	L	1-2	Hartson 14
16	Huddersfield Town (CCC 2-1)	A	L	0-1	
20	Newcastle United	H	L	0-1	
24	Arsenal	A	L	0-4	
27	Liverpool	H	W	2-1	Hartson 16, Berkovic 65
29	Huddersfield Town (CCC 2-2)	H	W	3-0	Hartson 31, 45, 77

Stan Lazaridis.
Philip Cole/Allsport

October

4	Southampton	A	L	0-4	
14	Aston Villa (CCC 3)	H	W	3-0	Hartson 9, 81, Lampard 17
18	Bolton	H	W	3-0	Berkovic 67, Hartson 77, 90
27	Leicester City	A	L	1-2	Berkovic 58

November

9	Chelsea	A	L	1-2	Hartson 85 (pen)
19	Walsall (CCC 4)	H	W	4-1	Lampard 15, 73, 74, Hartson 16
23	Leeds	A	L	1-3	Lampard 65
29	Aston Villa	H	W	2-1	Hartson 18, 48

December

3	Palace	H	W	4-1	Hartson 31, Berkovic 45, Unsworth 48, Lomas 71
6	Derby County	A	L	0-2	
13	Sheff Wed	H	W	1-0	Kitson 68
20	Blackburn	A	L	0-3	
26	Coventry City	H	W	1-0	Kitson 17
28	Wimbledon	A	W	2-1	Kimble 31 (og), Kitson 54

January

3	Emley (FAC 3)	H	W	2-1	Lampard 4, Hartson 82
6	Arsenal (CCC QF)	H	L	1-2	Abou 75
10	Barnsley	H	W	6-0	Lampard 5, Abou 31, 52, Moncur 57, Hartson 67, Lazaridis 90
17	Tottenham Hotspur	A	L	0-1	
25	Manchester City (FAC 4)	A	W	2-1	Berkovic 28, Lomas 76
31	Everton	H	D	2-2	Sinclair 10, 48

February

7	Newcastle United	A	W	1-0	Lazaridis 16
14	Blackburn Rovers (FAC 5)	H	D	2-2	Kitson 28, Berkovic 44
21	Bolton Wanderers	A	D	1-1	Sinclair 65
25	Blackburn Rovers (FAC 5R)	A	W	1-1	Hartson 103
	(Won 5-4 on penalties)				

March

2	Arsenal	H	D	0-0	
8	Arsenal (FAC 6)	A	D	1-1	Pearce 12
11	Manchester United	H	D	1-1	Sinclair 7
14	Chelsea	H	W	2-1	Sinclair 69, Unsworth 75
17	Arsenal (FAC 6R)	H	L	1-1	Hartson 84
	Lost 3-4 on penalties				
30	Leeds United	H	W	3-0	Hartson 8, Abou 23, Pearce 68

April

4	Aston Villa	A	L	0-2	
11	Derby County	H	D	0-0	
13	Sheffield Wednesday	A	D	1-1 Berkovic 7	
18	Blackburn Rovers	H	W	2-1	Hartson 7, 28
25	Southampton	H	L	2-4	Sinclair 42, Lomas 82

May

2	Liverpool	A	L	0-5	
5	Crystal Palace	A	D	3-3	Curcic 4 og, Omoyimni 68, 89
10	Leicester City	H	W	4-3	Lampard 15, Abou 31, 74, Sinclair 65

John Hartson. Gary M. Prior/Allsport

Squad

GOALKEEPERS
LUDECK MIKLOSKO
SHAKA HISLOP
CRAIG FORREST

DEFENDERS
TIM BREACKER   IAN PEARCE   SCOTT MEAN
RIO FERDINAND   RICHARD HALL

MIDFIELDERS
EMMANUEL OMOYIMNI   STEVE LOMAS   JOHN MONCUR   TREVOR SINCLAIR
ANDY IMPEY   STAN LAZARIDIS
EYAL BERKOVIC   FRANK LAMPARD JNR

STRIKERS
JOHN HARTSON   SAMASSI ABOU   PAUL KITSON
IAN WRIGHT

Samassi Abou
DOB: 4/4/73, Gabnoa, Ivory Coast
Signed: Cannes, (£400,000)
October 1997
League Debut: 9/11/97

Eyal Berkovic
DOB: 2/4/72, Haifa, Israel
Signed: Southampton,
(£1.75 million) June 1997
League Debut: 9/8/97

Tim Breacker
DOB: 2/7/65, Bicester
Signed: Oxford United, (£600,000)
October 1990
League Debut: 20/10/90

Rio Ferdinand
DOB: 7/11/78, London
Signed: Trainee, November 1995
League Debut: 5/5/96

Craig Forrest
DOB: 20/9/67, Vancouver, Canada
Signed: Ipswich Town, (£500,000)
July 1997
League Debut: 18/10/97

Richard Hall
DOB: 14/3/72, Ipswich
Signed: Southampton,
(£1.4 million) July 1996
League Debut: 9/4/97

John Hartson
DOB: 5/4/75, Swansea, Wales
Signed: Arsenal, (£3.2 million)
February 1997
League Debut: 15/2/97

Shaka Hislop
DOB: 22/2/69, London
Signed: Newcastle United, (free)
June 1998
League Debut: TBA

Andy Impey
DOB: 30/9/71, London
Signed: Queens Park Rangers,
(£1.3 million) June 1997
League Debut: 27/9/97

Paul Kitson
DOB: 9/1/71, Peterlee
Signed: Newcastle United,
(£2.3 million) February 1997
League Debut: 15/2/97

Frank Lampard
DOB: 20/6/78, Romford
Signed: Trainee
League Debut: 31/1/96

Stan Lazaridis
DOB: 16/8/72, Perth, Australia
Signed: W Adelaide, (£300,000)
September 1995
League Debut: 11/9/95

Steve Lomas
DOB: 18/1/74, Hanover,
Germany
Signed: Manchester City,
(£1.6 million) March 1997
League Debut: 9/4/97

Scott Mean
DOB: 13/12/73, Crawley
Signed: Bournemouth, 1997
League Debut: 30/3/98

John Moncur
DOB: 22/9/66, London
Signed: Swindon Town,
(£900,000) June 1994
League Debut: 27/8/94

Emmanuel Omoyimni
DOB: 28/12/77, Nigeria
Signed: Trainee
League Debut: 30/3/98

Ian Pearce
DOB: 7/5/74, Bury St Edmunds
Signed: Blackburn Rovers, 1997
League Debut: 20/9/97

Trevor Sinclair
DOB: 2/3/73, Dulwich
Signed: Queens Park Rangers,
(£3 million plus Iain Dowie and
Keith Rowland)
January 1998
League Debut: 31/1/98

1998-99 Premier League Fixtures

	Home	**Away**		**Home**	**Away**
Arsenal	6 Feb	26 Dec	Liverpool	12 Sep	20 Feb
Aston Villa	17 Oct	3 Apr	Manchester United	22 Aug	9 Jan
Blackburn Rovers	27 Feb	3 Oct	Middlesbrough	16 May	12 Dec
Charlton Athletic	5 Apr	24 Oct	Newcastle United	20 Mar	31 Oct
Chelsea	7 Nov	13 Mar	Nottingham Forest	13 Feb	19 Sep
Coventry City	28 Dec	29 Aug	Sheffield Wednesday	16 Jan	15 Aug
Derby County	17 Apr	21 Nov	Southampton	26 Sep	6 Mar
Everton	19 Dec	8 May	Tottenham Hotspur	28 Nov	24 Apr
Leeds United	1 May	5 Dec	Wimbledon	9 Sep	30 Jan
Leicester City	14 Nov	10 Apr			

Transfers In: Ian Wright (Arsenal £750,000), Marc Keller (Karlsruhe free), Shaka Hislop (Newcastle free), Javier Margas (Universidad Catolica £2m), Neil Rudduck (Liverpool £100,000)

Tranfers Out: Bernard Lama (PSG free), Mohammed Berthe (Bournemouth free)

Left: *Paul Kitson.*
Gary M. Prior/Allsport

Right: *Upton Park, home of West Ham United.*
Stu Forster/Allsport

PREMIER LEAGUE FOOTBALL

West Ham Utd

Derby County

Above: *Deon Burton.*
Graham Chadwick/Allsport

Right: *Paolo Wanchope.*
Graham Chadwick/Allsport

Mid-table mediocrity may suit some clubs who are just happy to live in the same division as the mighty, monied Arsenals, Liverpools, and Manchester Uniteds, but for Derby County, founder members of the Football League in 1888, and a club with a proud history, it is being seen as a springboard for greater honours.

Certainly at one stage of the season, it looked as if European action was a possibility, but a mediocre run-in—including eight losses in 12 games—meant that Europe would have to wait for another year. There's no doubting that when that day comes, Derby will not be overawed. The team can live with any opposition—especially the strikers who engineered a 3–0 thumping of Arsenal, a 3–1 victory against Blackburn Rovers, led Manchester United 2–0 (only to let it slip to 2–2 through two second-half defensive errors), and who also included the scalps of Liverpool and Newcastle amongst their 16 Premiership victories. Wanchope, Baiano and Sturridge converted 35 chances together this season—and that's more than many striking combinations managed in 1997-98.

The spell of Derby's greatest success can be pinpointed as the period of Brian Clough and Peter Taylor's management from the late 1960s when they returned to the top flight to take their first League title.

Early days saw them contest three FA Cup Finals in 1898, 1899 and 1903 and lose them all. They would have to wait until the first Cup Final after the Second World War to lay their hands on the prize, beating Charlton after extra time. The interwar period brought the club Third Division football for two seasons in 1955-57—the bottom had been reached.

Clough's 1967-73 reign changed all that. Having achieved the Second Division Championship in 1969 he built a team that took the League title three years later with stars like McFarland, Todd and Gemmill and formed the basis for a repeat performance three years later under Clough's captain turned manager, Dave Mackay.

Clough departed after a row with his chairman, and Derby subsided once more: a returning Peter Taylor couldn't stop the rot and their hundredth season was spent in the Third Division. Arthur Cox, Tony Docherty and Roy McFarland were among those given the opportunity to revive the Rams, but it wasn't until the arrival in 1995 of much-travelled Jim Smith, the 'Bald Eagle', that the investment of millionaire board member Lionel Pickering started to show rewards.

A multi-million pound move to Pride Park, a new ground outside the city centre, plus a multi-national team of Croatians, Costa Ricans and Italians ensure that Derby's place in the Premiership will be maintained in style.

Season at a Glance

1997-98 Final Position:	9th in the Premiership
Top League Goalscorers:	Wanchope: 13, Baiano: 12, Sturridge: 10
Highest League win:	5-2 v Sheffield Wed (A), 24 September 1997
Worst League Defeat:	0-5 v Leeds United (H), 15 March 1998
Highest Attendance:	30,492 v Liverpool, 10 May 1998
Lowest Attendance:	25,625 v Southampton, 27 September 1997

PREMIER LEAGUE FOOTBALL

Derby County

Managers

Harry Newbould	1900-06
Jimmy Methven	1906-22
Cecil Potter	1922-25
George Jobey	1925-41
Stuart McMillan	1946-53
Jack Barker	1953-55
Harry Storer	1955-62
Tim Ward	1962-67
Brian Clough	1967-73
Dave Mackay	1973-76
Colin Murphy	1976-77
Tommy Docherty	1977-79
Colin Addison	1979-82
John Newman	1982
Peter Taylor	1982-84
Roy McFarland	1984
Arthur Cox	1984-93
Roy McFarland	1993-95
Jim Smith	1995-

Above: *Manager Jim Smith.*
Mark Thompson/Allsport

Right: *Dean Sturridge.*
Ben Radford/Allsport

Honours

Division One Champions:	1971-72, 1974-75
Runners-up:	1895-96, 1929-30, 1935-36, 1995-96
Division Two Champions:	1911-12, 1914-15, 1968-69, 1986-87
Runners-up:	1925-26
Division Three (North) Champions:	1956-57
Runners-up:	1955-56
FA Cup Winners:	1946
Runners-up:	1898, 1899, 1903
Texaco Cup Winners:	1972
Football League Cup Winners:	1961, 1975, 1977, 1994, 1996
Runners-up:	1963, 1971
Anglo-Italian Cup Runners-up:	1993

Club Details

Year formed:	1884
Ground:	Pride Park Stadium, Derby DE24 8XL
Nickname:	The Rams
Club Colours:	White and black
Manager:	Jim Smith
Record attendance:	41,826 v Tottenham Hotspur, 20 September 1969, Division One
Record League victory:	9-0 v Wolverhampton Wanderers, 10 January 1891, Division One – Scorers: McMillan 5, Holmes 2, Roulston, Goodall; 9-0 v Sheffield Wednesday, 21 January 1899, Division One – Scorers: Bloomer 6, Oakden, McDonald, opposition own goal
Record Cup victory:	12-0 v Finn Harps, 15 September 1976, UEFA Cup First Round first leg – Scorers: Hector 5, George 3, James 3, Rioch
Record defeat:	2-11 v Everton, 18 January 1890, FA Cup First Round
Highest League scorer in a season:	Jack Bowers, 37, 1930-31, Division One; Ray Straw, 37, 1956-57, Division Three (North)
Highest League scorer during career:	Steve Bloomer, 292, 1892-1906, 1910-14
Most League appearances:	Kevin Hector, 486, 1966-78, 1980-82

Derby County

97/98 Results

August

9	Blackburn Rovers	A	L	0-1	
23	Tottenham Hotspur	A	L	0-1	
30	Barnsley	H	W	1-0	Eranio 43 (pen)

September

13	Everton	H	W	3-1	Hunt 23, C Powell 33, Sturridge 66
16	Southend United (CCC 2-1)	A	W	1-0	Wanchope 43
20	Aston Villa	A	L	1-2	Baiano 15
24	Sheffield Wednesday	A	W	5-2	Baiano 7, 48, Laursen 26, Wanchope 33, Burton 75
27	Southampton	H	W	4-0	Eranio 76 (pen), Wanchope 79, Baiano 82, Carsley 83

Dean Yates.
Mark Thompson/Allsport

October

1	Southend United (CCC 2-2)	H	W	5-0	Rowett 43, 57, Wanchope 60, Sturridge 64, Trollope 83
6	Leicester City	A	W	2-1	Baiano 21, 62
15	Spurs (CCC 3)	A	W	2-1	Wanchope 27, 71
18	Man U	H	D	2-2	Baiano 24, Wanchope 39
22	Wimbledon	H	D	1-1	Baiano 53
25	Liverpool	A	L	0-4	

November

1	Arsenal	H	W	3-0	Wanchope 46, 65, Sturridge 82
8	Leeds United	A	L	3-4	Sturridge 4, 11, Asanovic 33 (pen)
18	Newcastle United (CCC 4)	H	L	0-1	
22	Coventry City	H	W	3-1	Baiano 3, Eranio 30 (pen), Wanchope 39
29	Chelsea	A	L	0-4	

December

6	West Ham United	H	W	2-0	Sturridge 10, 49
14	Bolton Wanderers	A	D	3-3	Eranio 55, Baiano 64, 69
17	Newcastle United	A	D	0-0	
20	Crystal Palace	H	D	0-0	
26	Newcastle United	H	W	1-0	Eranio 4 (pen)
28	Barnsley	A	L	0-1	

January

3	Southampton (FAC 3)	H	W	2-0	Baiano 68 (pen), C Powell 73
11	Blackburn Rovers	H	W	3-1	Sturridge 15, 40, Wanchope 88
17	Wimbledon	A	D	0-0	
24	Coventry City (FAC 4)	A	L	0-2	
31	Spurs	H	W	2-1	Sturridge 25, Wanchope 77

February

7	Aston Villa	H	L	0-1	
14	Everton	A	W	2-1	Stimac 21, Wanchope 50
21	Man U	A	L	0-2	
28	Sheffield Wed	H	W	3-0	Wanchope 3, 49, Rowett 67

March

15	Leeds United	H	L	0-5	
28	Coventry City	A	L	0-1	

April

5	Chelsea	H	L	0-1	
11	West Ham United	A	D	0-0	
13	Bolton Wanderers	H	W	4-0	Wanchope 27, Burton 37, 40, Baiano 45
18	Crystal Palace	A	L	1-3	Bohinen
26	Leicester City	H	L	0-4	
29	Arsenal	A	L	0-1	

May

2	Southampton	A	W	2-0	Dailly 50, Sturridge 88
10	Liverpool	H	W	1-0	Wanchope 63

Stefano Eranio.
Mark Thompson/Allsport

PREMIER LEAGUE FOOTBALL

Derby County

Squad

GOALKEEPERS
MART POOM
RUSSELL HOULT

DEFENDERS
STEFANO ERANIO   HORACIO CARBONARI   JACOB LAURSEN
ROBERT KOZLUK   GARY ROWETT   STEFAN SCHNOOR
IGOR STIMAC

MIDFIELDERS
LEE CARSLEY   CHRISTIAN DAILLY   LARS BOHINEN   MAURICIO SOLIS

RORY DELAP   ROBBIE VAN DER LAAN   JONATHAN HUNT
PAULO WANCHOPE   DARRYL POWELL

STRIKERS
DEON BURTON   DEAN STURRIDGE   FRANCESCO BAIANO
RON WILLEMS

Francesco Baiano
DOB: 24/2/68, Naples, Italy
Signed: Fiorentina, (£650,000)
July 1997
League Debut: 30/8/97

Lars Bohinen
DOB: 8/9/66, Vadso, Norway
Signed: Blackburn Rovers,
March 1998
League Debut: 28/3/98

Deon Burton
DOB: 25/10/76, Reading
Signed: Portsmouth, (£1 million)
July 1997
League Debut: 9/8/97

Horacio Carbonari
DOB: Unknown, Argentina
Signed: Rosario Central, May 1998
League Debut: TBA

Lee Carsley
DOB: 28/2/74, Birmingham
Signed: Trainee, July 1992
League Debut: 11/9/94

Christian Dailly
DOB: 23/10/73, Dundee, Scotland
Signed: Dundee United, July 1996
League Debut: 17/8/96

Rory Delap
DOB: 6/7/76, Sutton Coldfield
Signed: Carlisle United,
February 1998
League Debut: 14/2/98

Stefano Eranio
DOB: 29/12/66, Genoa, Italy
Signed: AC Milan, (free)
June 1997
League Debut: 9/8/97

Jonathan Hunt
DOB: 2/11/71, London
Signed: Birmingham City,
(£500,000) June 1997
League Debut: 9/8/97

Robert Kozluk
DOB: 5/8/77, Mansfield
Signed: Trainee
League Debut: 25/10/97

Jacob Laursen
DOB: 6/10/71, Vejle, Denmark
Signed: Silkeborg, June 1996
League Debut: 17/8/96

Mart Poom
DOB: 3/2/72, Tallinn, Estonia
Signed: Flora Tallinn, March
1997
League Debut: 5/4/97

Darryl Powell
DOB: 15/1/71, Lambeth,
London
Signed: Portsmouth, (£750,000)
July 1995
League Debut: 13/8/95

Gary Rowett
DOB: 6/3/74, Bromsgrove
Signed: Everton, (£300,000)
July 1995
League Debut: 13/8/95

Stefan Schnoor
DOB: Unknown, Germany
Signed: SV Hamburg, (free)
June 1998
League Debut: TBA

Mauricio Solis
DOB: 13/12/72, Costa Rica
Signed: Herediano, March 1997
League Debut: 12/4/97

Igor Stimac
DOB: 6/9/67, Metkovic, Croatia
Signed: Hajduk Split,
(£1.57 million) October 1995
League Debut: 4/11/95

Dean Sturridge
DOB: 26/7/73, Birmingham
Signed: Trainee, July 1991
League Debut: 11/1/92

Robbie Van Der Laan
DOB: 5/9/68, Schiedam,
Holland
Signed: Port Vale, (£475,000)
August 1995
League Debut: 13/8/95

Paulo Wanchope
DOB: 31/1/76, Costa Rica
Signed: Herediano, March 1997
League Debut: 5/4/97

Ron Willems
DOB: 20/9/66, Epe, Holland
Signed: Grasshoppers Zurich,
(£300,000) July 1995
League Debut: 19/8/95

1998-99 Premier League Fixtures

	Home	Away		Home	Away
Arsenal	5 Dec	1 May	Manchester United	24 Oct	5 Apr
Aston Villa	6 Mar	26 Sep	Middlesbrough	28 Dec	29 Aug
Blackburn Rovers	16 Jan	15 Aug	Newcastle United	3 Apr	17 Oct
Charlton Athletic	20 Feb	12 Sep	Nottingham Forest	10 Apr	14 Nov
Chelsea	12 Dec	16 May	Sheffield Wednesday	9 Sep	30 Jan
Coventry City	8 May	19 Dec	Southampton	24 Apr	28 Nov
Everton	6 Feb	26 Dec	Tottenham Hotspur	3 Oct	27 Feb
Leeds United	31 Oct	20 Mar	West Ham United	21 Nov	17 Apr
Leicester City	19 Sep	13 Feb	Wimbledon	22 Aug	9 Jan
Liverpool	13 Mar	7 Nov			

Left: *Francesco Baiano.*
L. Griffiths/Allsport

Below: *Pride Park, home of Derby County.*
Mark Thompson/Allsport

Transfers In: Horacio Caronario (Rosario Central £2.7m), Stefan Schnoor (Hamburg free)
Tranfers Out: Chris Powell (Charlton £850,000), Robin van der Laan (Barnsley £325,000), Dean Yates (Watford free)

PREMIER LEAGUE FOOTBALL

Derby County

Leicester City

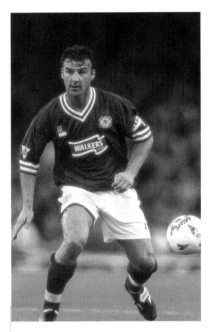

Above: *Steve Walsh.*
Graham
Chadwick/Allsport

Right: *Emile Heskey.*
Ross Kinnaird/
Allsport

Leicester City have established a long, proud record since their foundation in 1884 (as Leicester Fosse) and election to League Division Two a decade later. Yet the reputation they have had to live with is a club good enough to beat the best on their day, but lacking the resources or consistency to maintain a top-flight position. Their Filbert Street ground has been modernised to a high standard and their potential catchment area is certainly large enough to sustain a successful team.

The latest manager, appointed in late 1995, to build one was former Northern Ireland international Martin O'Neill, late of Wycombe and Norwich. He inherited a side that had just made its 18th transition between the top two divisions after just a single season in the élite under the managership of Brian Little. The nearest the club had come to the ultimate title was when they were shaded by Sheffield Wednesday in 1929.

O'Neill, however, quickly showed himself to be as good a manager as he had been a player and built a team based on a rock-like defence. Its 1997-98 record of only 41 goals conceded was only bettered by Champions Arsenal and runners-up Manchester United, and a number of teams that finished higher than Leicester in the Premiership must have looked covetously at O'Neill's defenders and at O'Neill himself, surely destined to become a big-club manager.

Despite a stingy defence, Leicester seemed to be involved in goalfests galore in the 1997-98 season: first there was the thrilling 3–3 draw at Highbury with three goals officially timed as being scored on 90 minutes—Leicester's first equaliser, Bergkamp's seeming winner for Arsenal and then Walsh's last gasp equaliser. Then there was the 3–5 loss to Blackburn, another 3–3 draw with Southampton and an end of season seven-goal epic when they lost 3–4 to the Hammers. And all this in a season when they beat Manchester United 1–0 away from home and Chelsea 2–0!

The biggest problem with Leicester in the past has been to hang on to its players, Gordon Banks, Peter Shilton, Frank Worthington, Alan Smith and Gary Lineker were among those to move on.

The arrival of O'Neill, one of the game's brightest young managers, helped turn Leicester into a genuine Premiership side, even though they arrived through the play-offs. A League (Coca-Cola) Cup win in 1997 took them into Europe, and the Foxes aimed to bury their reputation as a yo-yo team with internationals Elliott (Scotland), Keller (America) and Heskey (England Under 21) prominent in that cause.

Season at a Glance

1997-98 Final Position:	10th in the Premiership
Top League Goalscorers:	Heskey: 10, Elliott: 7, Marshall: 7
Highest League win:	4-0 v Derby County (A), 26 April 1998
Worst League Defeat:	3-5 v Blackburn (A), 28 February 1998
Highest Attendance:	21,699 v Newcastle United, 29 April 1998
Lowest Attendance:	18,553 v Wimbledon, 10 November 1997

PREMIER LEAGUE FOOTBALL

Leicester City

Managers

James Blessington	1907-09
Andy Aitken	1909-11
John Bartlett	1912-14
Peter Hodge	1919-26
Willie Orr	1926-32
Peter Hodge	1932-34
Arthur Lochhead	1934-36
Frank Womack	1936-39
Johnny Duncan	1946-49
Norman Bullock	1949-55
David Halliday	1955-58
Matt Gillies	1958-68
Frank O'Farrell	1968-71
Jimmy Bloomfield	1971-77
Frank McLintock	1977-78
Jock Wallace	1978-82
Gordon Milne	1982-86
Bryan Hamilton	1986-87
David Pleat	1987-91
Brian Little	1991-94
Mark McGhee	1994-95
Martin O'Neill	1995-

Above: *Manager Martin O'Neil.*
Ross Kinnaird/Allsport

Right: *Kasey Keller.*
Ben Radford/Allsport

Honours

Division One Runners-up:	1928-29
Division Two Champions:	1924-25, 1936-37, 1953-54, 1956-57, 1970-71, 1979-80
Runners-up:	1907-08
FA Cup Runners-up:	1949, 1961, 1963, 1969
Football League Cup Winners:	1964, 1997
Runners-up:	1965

Club Details

Year formed:	1884
Ground:	City Stadium, Filbert Street, Leicester LE2 7FL
Nickname:	The Fiberts or Foxes
Club Colours:	Blue
Manager:	Martin O'Neill
Record attendance:	47,298 v Tottenham Hotspur, 18 February 1928, FA Cup Fifth Round
Record League victory:	10-0 v Portsmouth, 20 October 1928, Division One – Scorers: Chandler 6, Hine 3, Barry
Record Cup victory:	8-1 v Coventry City, 1 December 1964, League Cup Fifth Round – Scorers: Norman 2, Hodgson 2, Stringfellow 2, Gibson, opposition own goal
Record defeat:	0-12 v Nottingham Forest, 21 April 1909, Division One (as Leicester Fosse)
Highest League scorer in a season:	Arthur Rowley, 44, 1956-57, Division Two
Highest League scorer during career:	Arthur Chandler, 259, 1923-35
Most League appearances:	Adam Black, 528, 1920-35

Leicester City

97/98 Results

August

9	Aston Villa	H	W	1-0	Marshall 37
13	Liverpool	A	W	2-1	Elliott 1, Fenton 83
23	Manchester United	H	D	0-0	
27	Arsenal	H	D	3-3	Heskey 84, Elliott 90, Walsh 90
30	Sheffield Wednesday	A	L	0-1	

September

13	Tottenham Hotspur	H	W	3-0	Walsh 55, Guppy 68, Heskey 77
16	Atletico Madrid (UEFA 1-1)	A	L	1-2	Marshall 11
20	Leeds United	A	W	1-0	Walsh 32
24	Blackburn Rovers	H	D	1-1	Izzet 43
27	Barnsley	A	W	2-0	Marshall 55, Fenton 63
30	Atletico Madrid (UEFA 1-2)	H	L	0-2	

Matt Elliott.
Mark Thompson/Allsport

October

6	Derby County	H	L	1-2	Elliott 67
14	Grimsby Town (CCC 3)	A	L	1-3	Marshall 17
18	Chelsea	A	L	0-1	
27	West Ham	H	W	2-1	Heskey 16, Marshall 82

November

1	Newcastle	A	D	3-3	Marshall 12, 32 Elliott 54
10	Wimbledon	H	L	0-1	
22	Bolton	H	D	0-0	
29	Coventry City	A	W	2-0	Fenton 32, Elliott 75 (pen)

December

6	Crystal Palace	H	D	1-1	Izzet 90
13	Southampton	A	L	1-2	Savage 84
20	Everton	H	L	0-1	
26	Arsenal	A	L	1-2	Lennon 77
28	Sheffield Wed	H	D	1-1	Guppy 28

January

3	Northampton (FAC 3)	H	W	4-0	Marshall 17, Parker 26 (pen), Savage 53, Cottee 58
10	Aston Villa	A	D	1-1	Parker 53 (pen)
17	Liverpool	H	D	0-0	
24	Crystal Palace (FAC 4)	A	L	0-3	
31	Man U	A	W	1-0	Cottee 30

February

7	Leeds United	H	W	1-0	Parker 44 (pen)
14	Spurs	A	D	1-1	Cottee 34
21	Chelsea	H	W	2-0	Heskey 3, 89
28	Blackburn Rovers	A	L	3-5	Wilson 68, Izzet 80, Ullathorne 81

March

14	Wimbledon	A	L	1-2	Savage 57
23	Man Utd	H	D	0-0	
28	Bolton	A	L	0-2	

April

4	Coventry City	H	D	1-1	Wilson 78
11	Crystal Palace	A	W	3-0	Heskey 45, 60, Elliott 74
14	Southampton	H	D	3-3	Lennon 18, Elliott 52, Parker 90 (pen)
18	Everton	A	D	1-1	Marshall 38
26	Derby County	A	W	4-0	Heskey 1, 8, Izzet 2, Marshall 15
29	Newcastle United	H	D	0-0	

May

2	Barnsley	H	W	1-0	Zagorakis 57
10	West Ham United	A	L	3-4	Cottee 59, 83, Heskey 66

Matt Elliott.
Mark Thompson/Allsport

PREMIER LEAGUE FOOTBALL

Leicester City

Squad

GOALKEEPERS
KASEY KELLER
PEGGUY ARPHEXAD

DEFENDERS
PONTUS KAAMARK   MATT ELLIOTT   IAN PEARCE   ROBERT   ULATHORNE
STUART CAMPBELL   JULIAN WATTS STEVE WALSH   SPENCER PRIOR
THEO ZAGORAKIS

MIDFIELDERS
GARRY PARKER MUZZY IZZET NEIL LENNON STEVE GUPPY
ROBBIE SAVAGE   SAM MCMAHON
SCOTT TAYLOR   STUART WILSON

STRIKERS
GRAHAM FENTON   EMILE HESKEY   IAN MARSHALL
TONY COTTEE   MARK ROBBINS

Pegguy Arphexad
DOB: Unknown, France
Signed: Lens, (free) July 1997
League Debut: 18/10/97

Stuart Campbell
DOB: 9/12/77, Corby
Signed: Trainee
League Debut: 30/11/96

Tony Cottee
DOB: 11/7/65, West Ham, London
Signed: Selangor, 1997
League Debut: 27/8/97

Matt Elliott
DOB: 1/11/68, Roehampton, London
Signed: Oxford United, (£1.6 million) January 1997
League Debut: 18/1/97

Graham Fenton
DOB: 22/5/74, Wallsend
Signed: Blackburn Rovers, 1997
League Debut: 13/8/97

Steve Guppy
DOB: 29/3/69, Winchester
Signed: Port Vale, (£850,000) February 1997
League Debut:1/3/97

Emile Heskey
DOB: 11/1/78, Leicester
Signed: Trainee
League Debut: 8/3/95

Muzzy Izzet
DOB:31/10/74, Mile End
Signed: Chelsea, (£650,000) July 1996
League Debut: 30/3/96

Pontus Kaamark
DOB: 5/4/69, Sweden
Signed: IFK Gothenburg, March 1997
League Debut: 22/3/97
Int'l Apps: Full Swedish

Kasey Keller
DOB: 27/1/69, Washington, USA
Signed: Millwall, (£900,000) August 1996
League Debut: 17/8/96

Neil Lennon
DOB: 25/6/71. Lurgan, N Ireland
Signed: Crewe, (£750,000) February 1996
League Debut: 24/2/96

Ian Marshall
DOB: 20/3/66, Liverpool
Signed: Ipswich Town, (£800,000) August 1996
League Debut: 2/9/96

Garry Parker
DOB: 7/9/65, Oxford
Signed: Aston Villa, (£300,000) February 1995
League Debut: 22/2/95

Spencer Prior
DOB: 22/4/71, Rochford
Signed: Norwich City, (£600,000) August 1996
League Debut: 17/8/96

Robbie Savage
DOB: 18/10/74, Wrexham
Signed: Crewe Alexandra, (£400,000) July 1997
League Debut: 9/8/97

Scott Taylor
DOB: 28/11/70, Portsmouth
Signed: Reading, (£500,000) July 1995
League Debut: 12/8/95

Steve Walsh
DOB: 3/11/64, Preston
Signed: Wigan Athletic, (£100,000) June 1986
League Debut: 23/8/86

Julian Watts
DOB: 17/3/71, Sheffield
Signed: Sheffield Wednesday, (£210,000) March 1996
League Debut: 30/3/96

Stuart Wilson
DOB: 16/9/77, Leicester
Signed: Trainee
League Debut: 22/2/97

Theo Zagorakis
DOB: 17/10/71, Greece
Signed: PAOK Salonika, 1998
League Debut: 7/2/98

1998-99 Premier League Fixtures

	Home	Away		Home	Away
Arsenal	12 Sep	20 Feb	Manchester United	16 Jan	15 Aug
Aston Villa	5 Apr	24 Oct	Middlesbrough	9 Sep	30 Jan
Blackburn Rovers	28 Dec	29 Aug	Newcastle United	8 May	19 Dec
Charlton Athletic	13 Mar	7 Nov	Nottingham Forest	12 Dec	16 May
Chelsea	21 Nov	17 Apr	Sheffield Wednesday	6 Feb	26 Dec
Coventry City	24 Apr	28 Nov	Southampton	5 Dec	1 May
Derby County	13 Feb	19 Sep	Tottenham Hotspur	17 Oct	3 Apr
Everton	22 Aug	9 Jan	West Ham United	10 Apr	14 Nov
Leeds United	27 Feb	3 Oct	Wimbledon	26 Sep	6 Mar
Liverpool	31 Oct	20 Mar			

Left: *Neil Lennon.*
Allsport

Transfers In: Gerry Taggart (Bolton free)
Tranfers Out: None

Below: *Muzzy Izzet.*
Allsport

PREMIER LEAGUE FOOTBALL

Leicester City

Coventry City

Above: *Darren Huckerby.*
Stu Forster/Allsport

Right: *Dion Dublin.*
Phil Cole/Allsport

Coventry in 1997-98 were the Premiership's draw specialists—they enjoyed 16 of them during the campaign and only 10 losses, the fourth fewest losses after the top three, Arsenal, Man U and Liverpool. An excellent goals against record—44, sixth best—confirmed their defensive abilities, but apart from Dion Dublin, whose 18 goals earned him an England call-up, and lightning-quick England hopeful Darren Huckerby (14), too few chances were converted to enable Gordon Strachan's team seriously to vie for honours.

They certainly started and finished well. An opening season rout of Championship contenders Chelsea thanks to a Dublin hat-trick, however, was followed by a mediocre season till Christmas. The 3–2 victory over Manchester United on 28 December (courtesy 86th and 88th minute goals from Dublin and Huckerby) saw their fortunes change. They would only lose three games from then, one of those on penalties to Sheffield United in the FA cup. There were 12 wins—seven of them in succession—and a sense of what might have been had a few more midfield chances gone in.

Elected to Division Two after the First World War, Coventry City seemed unlikely candidates for the top flight, yet they emerged to climb to Division One in 1967, and remained there for the best part of the next three decades, thanks to the management team of Jimmy Hill and Derrick Robins, who took the reins in 1961. As manager and chairman, they'd preside over the club's most successful period in history. Adopting a new Sky Blue strip, they attempted many different marketing strategies to sell soccer to the 1960s' public, many of which were far-sighted including radio stations and special trains to away matches. Hill achieved success on the pitch with a team featuring the likes of keeper Bill Glazier, defender Mick Kearns and inspirational captain George Curtis.

Maintaining their top-flight status is enough for most Coventry fans, enjoying the opulence of Highfield Road which became the League's first all-seater stadium. But though they have never mounted a serious title challenge (their highest finish is sixth) there was the occasional Cup run – most notably in 1987, when the FA Cup was obtained after a 3-2 extra-time thriller with hot favourites Spurs.

Jimmy Hill was of course long gone to TV punditry, managers in the meanwhile included Ron Atkinson, appointed in 1995, who brought with him Gordon Strachan as his assistant. Strachan succeeded Atkinson in 1996 and brought off a last-gasp rescue act. Relegation was avoided with ease in 1997-98, Dion Dublin leading from the front (and occasionally back) to become the club's first England international for many years.

Season at a Glance

1997-98 Final Position:	11th in the Premiership
Top League Goalscorers:	Dublin: 18, Huckerby: 14, Whelan: 6
Highest League win:	5-1 v Bolton (A), 31 January 1998
Worst League Defeat:	0-3 v Man United (A), 30 August 1998
	0-3 v Aston Villa (A), 6 December 1997
Highest Attendance:	23,054 v Man United, 28 December 1997
Lowest Attendance:	15,900 v Crystal Palace, 24 September 1997

Coventry City

Managers

Above: *Manager Gordon Strachan.*
Phil Cole/Allsport

Right: *George Boateng tackles Paul Ince.*
Stu Forster/Allsport

William Clayton	1919
Harry Pollitt	1919-20
Albert Evans	1920-24
James Kerr	1925-28
James McIntyre	1928-31
Harry Storer	1931-45
Dick Bayliss	1945-47
Billy Frith	1947-48
Harry Storer	1948-53
Jack Fairbrother	1953-54
Charlie Elliott	1954-55
Jesse Carver	1955
George Raynor	1956
Harry Warren	1956-57
Billy Frith	1957-61
Jimmy Hill	1961-67
Noel Cantwell	1967-72
Gordon Milne	1972-81
Dave Sexton	1981-83
Bobby Gould	1983-84
Don Mackay	1984-86
George Curtis	1986-87
John Sillett	1987-90
Terry Butcher	1990-92
Don Howe	1992
Bobby Gould	1992-93
Phil Neal	1993-95
Ron Atkinson	1995-96
Gordon Strachan	1996-

Honours

Division Two Champions:	1966-67
Division Three (South) Champions:	1935-36
Division Three Champions:	1963-64
Runners-up:	1925-26
Division Four Runners-up:	1958-59
FA Cup Winners:	1987

Club Details

Year formed:	1883
Ground:	Highfield Road Stadium, King Richard Street, Coventry CV2 4FW
Nickname:	The Sky Blues
Club Colours:	Sky blue
Manager:	Gordon Strachan
Record attendance:	51,455 v Wolverhampton Wanderers, 29 April 1967, Division Two
Record League victory:	9-0 v Bristol City, 28 April 1934, Division Three (South) – Scorers: Bourton 5, White 2, Jones 2
Record Cup victory:	7-0 v Scunthorpe United, 24 November 1934, FA Cup First Round – Scorers: Birtley 2, Lauderdale 2, Bourton, Jones, Liddle
Record defeat:	2-10 v Norwich City, 15 March 1930, Division Three (South)
Highest League scorer in a season:	Clarrie Bourton, 49, 1931-32, Division Three (South)
Highest League scorer during career:	Clarrie Bourton, 171, 1931-37
Most League appearances:	George Curtis, 486, 1956-70

97/98 Results

August

9	Chelsea	H	W	3-2	Dublin 41, 82, 88
11	Arsenal	A	L	0-2	
23	Bolton Wanderers	H	D	2-2	Telfer 8, Huckerby 20
27	West Ham United	H	D	1-1	Huckerby 38
30	Manchester United	A	L	0-3	

September

13	Southampton	H	W	1-0	Soltvedt 65
16	Blackpool (CCC 2-1)	A	L	0-1	
20	Sheffield Wednesday	A	D	0-0	
24	Crystal Palace	H	D	1-1	Dublin 8
28	Blackburn Rovers	A	D	0-0	

Noel Whelan.
Stu Forster/Allsport

October

1	Blackpool (CCC 2-2)	H	W	3-1	McAllister 61 (pen), 89 (pen), Dublin 70
4	Leeds United	H	D	0-0	
15	Everton (CCC 3)	H	W	4-1	Hall 6, Salako 33, 59, Haworth 62
20	Barnsley	A	L	0-2	
25	Everton	H	D	0-0	

November

1	Wimbledon	A	W	2-1	Huckerby 17, Dublin 22
8	Newcastle	H	D	2-2	Dublin 4, 82
18	Arsenal (CCC 4)	A	L	0-1	
22	Derby County	A	L	1-3	Huckerby 71
29	Leicester City	H	L	0-2	

December

6	Aston Villa	A	L	0-3	
13	Spurs	H	W	4-0	Huckerby 42, 84, Breen 63, Hall 87
20	Liverpool	A	L	0-1	
26	West Ham	A	L	0-1	
28	Man U	H	W	3-2	Whelan 12, Dublin 86 (pen), Huckerby 88

January

3	Liverpool (FAC 3)	A	W	3-1	Huckerby 45, Dublin 62, Telfer 87
10	Chelsea	A	L	1-3	Telfer 30
17	Arsenal	H	D	2-2	Whelan 21, Dublin 66 (pen)
24	Derby County (FAC 4)	H	W	2-0	Dublin 38, 45
31	Bolton Wanderers	A	W	5-1	Whelan 26, Huckerby 58, 65, Dublin 73, 79

February

7	Sheffield Wed	H	W	1-0	Dublin 74 (pen)
14	Aston Villa (FAC 5)	A	W	1-0	Moldovan 72
18	Southampton	A	W	2-1	Whelan 14, Huckerby 29
21	Barnsley	H	W	1-0	Dublin 89 (pen)
28	Crystal Palace	A	W	3-0	Telfer 1, Moldovan 40, Dublin 77

March

7	Sheffield United (FAC 6)	H	D	1-1	Dublin 32 (pen)
14	Newcastle United	A	D	0-0	
17	Sheffield United (FAC 6R)	A	L	1-1	Telfer 10
	(Lost 1-3 on penalties)				
28	Derby County	H	W	1-0	Huckerby 44

April

4	Leicester City	A	D	1-1	Whelan 80
11	Aston Villa	H	L	1-2	Whelan 59
13	Tottenham Hotspur	A	D	1-1	Dublin 86
19	Liverpool	H	D	1-1	Dublin 47 (pen)
25	Leeds United	A	D	3-3	Huckerby 20, 34, 62
29	Wimbledon	H	D	0-0	

May

2	Blackburn Rovers	H	W	2-0	Dublin 19 (pen), Boateng 34
10	Everton	A	D	1-1	Dublin 89

Gary McAllister.
Ben Radford/Allsport

113

PREMIER LEAGUE FOOTBALL

Squad

GOALKEEPERS
STEVE OGRIZOVIC
MAGNUS HEDMAN

DEFENDERS
PAUL WILLIAMS   GARY BREEN   DAVID BURROWS
ROLAND NILSSON   LIAM DAISH   MARCUS HALL
BRIAN BORROWS   RICHARD SHAW

MIDFIELDERS
PAUL TELFER   GEORGE BOATENG   GARY McALLISTER   JOHN SALAKO

MICHAEL O'NEILL   TRONDT EGIL SOLTVEDT   NOEL WHELAN
WILLIE BOLAND   GAVIN STRACHAN

STRIKERS
VIOREL MOLDOVAN   DION DUBLIN   DARREN HUCKERBY
MARTIN JOHANSEN

Francesco Baiano
DOB: 24/2/68, Naples, Italy
Signed: Fiorentina, (£650,000)
July 1997
League Debut: 30/8/97

Lars Bohinen
DOB: 8/9/66, Vadso, Norway
Signed: Blackburn Rovers,
March 1998
League Debut: 28/3/98

Deon Burton
DOB: 25/10/76, Reading
Signed: Portsmouth, (£1 million)
July 1997
League Debut: 9/8/97

Horacio Carbonari
DOB: Unknown, Argentina
Signed: Rosario Central,
May 1998
League Debut: TBA

Lee Carsley
DOB: 28/2/74, Birmingham
Signed: Trainee, July 1992
League Debut: 11/9/94

Christian Dailly
DOB: 23/10/73, Dundee, Scotland
Signed: Dundee United,
July 1996
League Debut: 17/8/96

Rory Delap
DOB: 6/7/76, SuttonColdfield
Signed: Carlisle United,
February 1998
League Debut: 14/2/98

Stefano Eranio
DOB: 29/12/66, Genoa, Italy
Signed: AC Milan, (free)
June 1997
League Debut: 9/8/97

Jonathan Hunt
DOB: 2/11/71, London
Signed: Birmingham City,
(£500,000) June 1997
League Debut: 9/8/97

Robert Kozluk
DOB: 5/8/77, Mansfield
Signed: Trainee
League Debut: 25/10/97

Jacob Laursen
DOB: 6/10/71, Vejle, Denmark
Signed: Silkeborg, June 1996
League Debut: 17/8/96

Mart Poom
DOB: 3/2/72, Tallinn, Estonia
Signed: Flora Tallinn,
March 1997
League Debut: 5/4/97

Darryl Powell
DOB: 15/1/71, Lambeth,
London
Signed: Portsmouth, (£750,000)
July 1995
League Debut: 13/8/95

Gary Rowett
DOB: 6/3/74, Bromsgrove
Signed: Everton, (£300,000)
July 1995
League Debut: 13/8/95

Stefan Schnoor
DOB: Unknown, Germany
Signed: SV Hamburg, (free)
June 1998
League Debut: TBA

Mauricio Solis
DOB: 13/12/72, Costa Rica
Signed: Herediano,
March 1997
League Debut: 12/4/97

Igor Stimac
DOB: 6/9/67, Metkovic, Croatia
Signed: Hajduk Split,
(£1.57 million) October 1995
League Debut: 4/11/95

Dean Sturridge
DOB: 26/7/73, Birmingham
Signed: Trainee, July 1991
League Debut: 11/1/92

Robbie Van Der Laan
DOB: 5/9/68, Schiedam,
Holland
Signed: Port Vale, (£475,000)
August 1995
League Debut: 13/8/95

Paulo Wanchope
DOB: 31/1/76, Costa Rica
Signed: Herediano, March 1997
League Debut: 5/4/97

Ron Willems
DOB: 20/9/66, Epe, Holland
Signed: Grasshoppers Zurich,
(£300,000) July 1995
League Debut: 19/8/95

1998-99 Premier League Fixtures

	Home	Away		Home	Away
Arsenal	5 Dec	1 May	Manchester United	24 Oct	5 Apr
Aston Villa	6 Mar	26 Sep	Middlesbrough	28 Dec	29 Aug
Blackburn Rovers	16 Jan	15 Aug	Newcastle United	3 Apr	17 Oct
Charlton Athletic	20 Feb	12 Sep	Nottingham Forest	10 Apr	14 Nov
Chelsea	12 Dec	16 May	Sheffield Wednesday	9 Sep	30 Jan
Coventry City	8 May	19 Dec	Southampton	24 Apr	28 Nov
Everton	6 Feb	26 Dec	Tottenham Hotspur	3 Oct	27 Feb
Leeds United	31 Oct	20 Mar	West Ham United	21 Nov	17 Apr
Leicester City	19 Sep	13 Feb	Wimbledon	22 Aug	9 Jan
Liverpool	13 Mar	7 Nov			

Left: *John Salako.*
Clive Brunskill/
Allsport

Below: *Coventry celebrate the 1–1 draw with Liverpool.*
Clive Brunskill/
Allsport

Transfers In: Jean-Guy Wallemme (Lens £750,000), Ian Brightwell (Man City free)
Tranfers Out: Viorel Moldovan (Fenerbache £4.5m), John Salako (Fulham free)

PREMIER LEAGUE FOOTBALL

Coventry City

Southampton

Above: *Matt le Tissier.*
Dan Smith/Allsport

Right: *Egil Ostenstad.*
Phil Cole/Allsport

When you lose seven of your first ten games, it's unlikely that you are going to be in contention for top honours—so Saints' fans knew what to expect as the 1997-98 season got underway. It seemed likely that, as has been the case for some years, Southampton would be fighting for survival. But as the season wore on, it became apparent that David Jones' unglamorous but efficient style of management was having great effect and the team was gelling.

Any team that can boast victories against Manchester United (1–0), Liverpool (3–2), Chelsea (1–0), Leeds (1–0) and Blackburn (3–0)—in other words against all the clubs in the first six of the Premiership except champions Arsenal, has got something. Apart from the enigmatic skills of Matt Le Tissier, whose form improved from a mid-season slump, Southampton could point to the gangling efforts of Carlton Palmer, the professionalism of Kevin Richardson, and a trio of goalscorers in Ostenstad, Hirst, and young Kevin Davies who between them notched nearly 30 chances.

The sale of the latter to Blackburn for £7.25 million has enabled Jones to strengthen his squad further and with Stuart Ripley supplying the crosses for Mark Hughes, and David Howells strengthening the midfield, the successes of 1997-98 could be a springboard.

Founded by church goers in 1885 as Southampton St Mary's (hence the club's nickname of the 'Saints'), the club became founder-members of the newly-created Third Division in 1920. Their early days had not been devoid of achievement but the upturn in fortunes came at the end of the 1950s when an impressive side finally won promotion to the First Division in 1966, consistent performances from international forwards Terry Paine, Ron Davies, Martin Chivers and later Mick Channon maintaining the momentum.

Lawrie McMenemy took over in 1974 and his flamboyant style and policy of bringing top players like Peter Shilton, Kevin Keegan and Alan Ball to the Dell paid off, with a victory against all the odds over Manchester United in the 1976 FA Cup Final preceding promotion back to the First Division in 1978.

Since then, Southampton have remained solidly in the top flight, despite failing to keep highly-talented youngsters like Alan Shearer, Rod Wallace and Tim Flowers along the way. The late 1990s brought progress in several respects: the old board sold out and manager David Jones arrived from Stockport, steering the previously struggling Saints to a respectable 12th in his first season in charge.

Season at a Glance

1997-98 Final Position:	12th in the Premiership
Top League Goalscorers:	Le Tissier: 11, Ostenstad: 11, Davies: 9, Hirst: 9
Highest League win:	4-1 v Barnsley (H), 8 November 1997
Worst League Defeat:	0-4 v Derby County (A), 27 September 1997
Highest Attendance:	15,255 v Spurs, 25 October 1997
Lowest Attendance:	14,815 v Wimbledon, 11 April 1998

PREMIER LEAGUE FOOTBALL

Southampton

Managers

James McIntyre	1919-24
Arthur Chadwick	1925-31
George Kay	1931-36
George Cross	1936-37
Tom Parker	1937-43
JR Sarjanston	1943-47
Bill Dodgin Snr	1946-49
Syd Cann	1949-51
George Roughton	1952-55
Ted Bates	1955-73
Lawrie McMenemy	1973-85
Chris Nicholl	1985-91
Ian Branfoot	1991-94
Alan Ball	1994-95
Dave Merrington	1995-96
Graeme Souness	1996-97
Dave Jones	1997-

Above: *Dave Jones.*
Dave Rogers/Allsport

Right: *Paul Jones.*
Phil Cole/Allsport

Honours

Division One Runners-up:	1983-84
Division Two Runners-up:	1965-66, 1977-78
Division Three (South) Champions:	1921-22
Runners-up:	1920-21
FA Cup Winners:	1976
Runners-up:	1900, 1902
Football League Cup Runners-up:	1979
Zenith Data Systems Cup Runners-up:	1992

Club Details

Year formed:	1885
Ground:	The Dell, Milton Road, Southampton SO9 4XX
Nickname:	The Saints
Club Colours:	Red, white and black
Manager:	Dave Jones
Record attendance:	31,044 v Manchester United, 8 October 1969, Division One
Record League victory:	9-3 v Wolverhampton Wanderers, 18 September 1965, Division Two – Scorers: Chivers 4, Paine 2, Sydenham 2, O'Brien
Record Cup victory:	7-1 v Ipswich Town, 7 January 1961, FA Cup Third Round – O'Brien 3 (1 pen), Mulgrew 2, Paine, Penk
Record defeat:	0-8 v Tottenham Hotspur, 28 March 1936, Division Two;
Highest League scorer in a season:	Derek Reeves, 39, 1959-60, Division Three
Highest League scorer during career:	Mike Channon, 185, 1966-77, 1979-82
Most League appearances:	Terry Paine, 713, 1956-74

Southampton

97/98 Results

August

9	Bolton Wanderers	H	L	0-1	
13	Manchester United	A	L	0-1	
23	Arsenal	H	L	1-3	Maddison 25
27	Crystal Palace	H	W	1-0	Davies 57
30	Chelsea	A	L	2-4	Davies 25, Monkou 59

September

13	Coventry City	A	L	0-1	
17	Brentford (CCC 2-1)	H	W	3-1	Monkou 37, Davies 60, Evans 69
20	Liverpool	H	D	1-1	Davies 48
24	Leeds United	H	L	0-2	
27	Derby County	A	L	0-4	
30	Brentford (CCC 2-2)	A	W	2-0	Le Tissier 31, 44

Carlton Palmer.
Ben Radford/Allsport

October

4	West Ham	H	W	3-0	Ostenstad 54, Davies 65, Dodd 68
14	Barnsley (CCC 3)	A	W	2-1	Le Tissier 15, Davies 88
18	Blackburn	A	L	0-1	
25	Spurs	H	W	3-2	Vega 54 (og), Hirst 67, 80

November

2	Everton	A	W	2-0	Le Tissier 24, Davies 54
8	Barnsley	H	W	4-1	Le Tissier 3 (pen), Palmer 5, Davies 35, Hirst 54
19	Chelsea (CCC 4)	A	L	1-2	Davies 52
22	Newcastle	A	L	1-2	Davies 5
29	Sheffield	H	L	2-3	Hirst 48, Palmer 55

December

7	Wimbledon	A	L	0-1	
13	Leicester	H	W	2-1	Le Tissier 2, Benali 54
20	Villa	A	D	1-1	Ostenstad 72
26	Palace	A	D	1-1	Oakley 39
29	Chelsea	H	W	1-0	Davies 16

January

3	Derby County (FAC 3)	A	L	0-2	
10	Bolton	A	D	0-0	
19	Man Utd	H	W	1-0	Davies 3
31	Arsenal	A	L	0-3	

February

7	Liverpool	A	W	3-2	Hirst 8 (pen), 90, Ostenstad 85
18	Coventry	H	L	1-2	Le Tissier 79 (pen)
21	Blackburn	H	W	3-0	Ostenstad 19, 88, Hirst 78
28	Leeds United	A	W	1-0	Hirst 54

March

7	Everton	H	W	2-1	Le Tissier 69 (pen), Ostenstad 86
14	Barnsley	A	L	3-4	Ostenstad 25, Le Tissier 41, 71
28	Newcastle	H	W	2-1	Pearce 69 og, Le Tissier 85 (pen)

April

4	Sheffield	A	L	0-1	
11	Wimbledon	H	L	0-1	
14	Leicester City	A	D	3-3	Ostenstad 17, 27, Hirst 49
18	Aston Villa	H	L	1-2	Le Tissier 19
25	West Ham	A	W	4-2	Le Tissier 40, Ostenstad 63, 86, Palmer 80

May

2	Derby County	H	L	0-2	
10	Spurs	A	D	1-1	Le Tissier 21

David Howells while still at Spurs.
Alex Livesey/Allsport

PREMIER LEAGUE FOOTBALL

Squad

GOALKEEPERS
PAUL JONES
NEIL MOSS
DARRYL FLAHAVAN

DEFENDERS
JASON DODD   KEN MONKOU   CARLTON PALMER   FRANCIS BENALI
CLAUS LUNDEKVAM   RICHARD DRYDEN   LEE TODD

MIDFIELDERS
MATTHEW OAKLEY   MATTHEW LE TISSIER   DAVID HUGHES   JOHN BERESFORD
STEVE BASHAM   DAVID HOWELLS   MATT ROBINSON
STUART RIPLEY   KEVIN RICHARDSON   JASON BOWEN

STRIKERS
STIG JOHANSEN   DAVID HIRST   EGIL OSTENSTAD
MARK HUGHES   ANDY WILLIAMS
JAMIE BEATTIE

Steve Basham
DOB: 2/12/77, London
Signed: Trainee
League Debut: 18/8/96

Francis Benali
DOB: 30/12/68, Southampton
Signed: Apprentice, January 1987
League Debut: 1/10/88

John Beresford
DOB: 4/9/66, Sheffield
Signed: Newcastle United,
(£1.5 million) February 1998
League Debut: 7/2/98

Jason Dodd
DOB: 2/11/70, Bath
Signed: Bath City, (£50,000)
March 1989
League Debut: 14/10/89

Richard Dryden
DOB: 14/6/69, Stroud
Signed: Bristol City, (£150,000)
August 1996
League Debut: 18/8/96

David Hirst
DOB: 7/12/67, Cudworth
Signed: Sheffield Wednesday, (£2
million) October 1997
League Debut: 18/10/97

David Hughes
DOB: 2/8/74, St Albans
Signed: Trainee, July 1991
League Debut: 5/2/94

Stig Johansen
DOB: 13/6/72, Norway
Signed: Bodo Glimt, (£600,000)
August 1997
League Debut: TBA

Paul Jones
DOB: 18/4/67, Chirk
Signed: Stockport County,
(£800,000) July 1997
League Debut: 9/8/97

Matthew Le Tissier
DOB: 14/10/68, Guernsey
Signed: Apprentice,
October 1986
League Debut: 30/8/86

Claus Lundekvam
DOB: 22/2/73, Norway
Signed: Brann, (£400,000)
September 1996
League Debut: 4/9/96

Ken Monkou
DOB: 29/11/64, Surinam
Signed: Chelsea, (£750,000)
August 1992
League Debut: 24/8/92

Neil Moss
DOB: 10/5/75, New Milton
Signed: Bournemouth,
(£250,000) December 1995
League Debut: 4/9/96

Matthew Oakley
DOB: 17/8/77, Peterborough
Signed: Trainee, July 1995
League Debut: 6/5/95

Egil Ostenstad
DOB: 2/1/72, Haugesund,
Norway
Signed: Viking, (£900,000)
October 1996
League Debut: 13/10/96

Carlton Palmer
DOB: 5/12/65, Rowley Regis
Signed: Leeds United,
(£2.6 million) September 1997
League Debut: 27/9/97

Kevin Richardson
DOB: 4/12/62, Newcastle
Signed: Coventry City,
(£150,000) September 1997
League Debut: 13/9/97

Stuart Ripley
DOB: 20/11/67,
Middelsbrough
Signed: Blackburn Rovers,
(free) June 1998
League Debut: TBA

Andy Williams
DOB: 8/10/77, Bristol
Signed: Trainee
League Debut: 9/8/97

1998-99 Premier League Fixtures

	Home	Away		Home	Away
Arsenal	3 Apr	17 Oct	Liverpool	15 Aug	16 Jan
Aston Villa	14 Nov	10 Apr	Manchester United	3 Oct	27 Feb
Blackburn Rovers	17 Apr	21 Nov	Middlesbrough	7 Nov	13 Mar
Charlton Athletic	9 Jan	22 Aug	Newcastle United	20 Feb	12 Sep
Chelsea	26 Dec	6 Feb	Nottingham Forest	29 Aug	28 Dec
Coventry City	24 Oct	5 Apr	Sheffield Wednesday	20 Mar	31 Oct
Derby County	28 Nov	24 Apr	Tottenham Hotspur	19 Sep	13 Feb
Everton	16 May	12 Dec	West Ham United	6 Mar	26 Sep
Leeds United	30 Jan	8 Sep	Wimbledon	19 Dec	8 May
Leicester City	1 May	5 Dec			

Transfers In: Stuart Ripley (Blackburn £1.5m), Jamie Beattie (Blackburn £800,000)
Mark Hughes (Chelsea £650,000), David Howells (Spurs free), Scot Marshall (Arsenal free),
Mark Paul (King's Lynn £75,000)
Tranfers Out: Kevin Davis (Blackburn £7.5m), Kevin Richardson Barnsley £500,000),
Duncan Spedding (Northampton £100,000), Lee Todd (Bradford City £250,000)

Left: *New Signing Mark Hughes in Chelsea colours.*
Ben Radford/Allsport

Below: *Players celebrating Dodd's goal.*
Ben Radford/Allsport

PREMIER LEAGUE FOOTBALL

Newcastle United

Above: *Shay Given.*
Stu Forster/Allsport

Right: *Alan Shearer.*
Graham Chadwick/Allsport

On 17 September 1997, after defeating Spanish giants Barcelona 3–2 in a pulsating game, the St James' Park crowd sang their way home looking forward to a season when, surely, the almosts and maybes would be over.

No such luck. Problems off the pitch mirrored the problems on it and, apart from a cup run that ended in such disappointment at Wembley against all-conquering Arsenal, the Magpies' season was a disaster. Losing England's best striker to injury didn't help: Alan Shearer's convalescence left the £15 million man on the sidelines for most of the season, and when he did come back there were signs that he'd need a while to play himself into form. It's certainly been a long time since he was only worth two goals in a league season, and even four goals in the cup couldn't hide his frustration.

What a difference Shearer fit would have made! With John Barnes Newcastle's top scorer with six Premiership goals, and Tino Asprilla, who scored six in the first six matches, including a corruscating hat-trick against Barcelona, leaving the club, the Magpies averaged less than a goal a game in the Premiership. They could only manage 35 all season, fewer than any of the relegated sides and only a professional defence—whose 44 goals against put them sixth best in the league—kept the team away from the First Division.

There's no doubt at all that 1998-99 will have to be a whole lot better and the Geordies must be looking forward to seeing Frenchman Stephane Guivarc'h, who got into so many good goal-scoring positions during the World Cup Final against Brazil, partnering a fit Alan Shearer up front.

United's impressive pedigree is based on two periods of achievement, the first between 1905 and 1911 when they won the League Championship three times and won the FA Cup in 1910. The second spell saw three FA Cup victories in six seasons in the 1950s. But the break-up of this team marked the beginning of a search for consistency which has continued to this day. There were flashes of inspiration, and Magpies' fans will remember the likes of Bobby Moncur, 'Pop' Robson and Malcolm Macdonald with affection. Although the European Fairs Cup came to St James' Park in 1969, the nearest they came to a domestic honour was a miserable showing against Liverpool in the 1974 FA Cup Final.

Kevin Keegan's arrival as manager started the renaissance, and with top-flight status regained the following season, the stage seemed set for a return to the glory days of old. But two runners-up spots in the Premiership and an FA Cup Final appearance proved scant reward for the investment and Keegan was replaced by Kenny Dalglish whose less entertaining brand of football hasn't yet provided Tyneside with the success it craves.

Season at a Glance

1997-98 Final Position:	13th, Premiership
Top League Goalscorers:	Barnes: 6, Lee: 4, Gillespie: 4
Highest League win:	3-1 v Chelsea (H), 2 May 1998
Worst League Defeat:	1-4 v Leeds United (A), 18 October 1997
Highest Attendance:	36,783 v Aston Villa, 23 August 1997
Lowest Attendance:	36,289 v Derby County, 17 December 1997

PREMIER LEAGUE FOOTBALL

Managers

Andy Cunningham	1930-35
Tom Mather	1935-39
Stan Seymour	1939-47
George Martin	1947-50
Stan Seymour	1950-54
Dug Livingstone	1954-56
Charlie Mitten	1958-61
Norman Smith	1961-62
Joe Harvey	1962-75
Gordon Lee	1975-77
Richard Dinnis	1977
Bill McGarry	1977-80
Arthur Cox	1980-84
Jack Charlton	1984-85
Willie McFaul	1985-88
Jim Smith	1988-91
Ossie Ardiles	1991-92
Kevin Keegan	1992-97
Kenny Dalglish	1997-

Above: *Manager Kenny Dalglish.*
Stu Forster/Allsport

Right: *Nikos Dabizas.*
Stu Forster/Allsport

Club Details

Year formed:	1881
Ground:	St James' Park, Newcastle-upon-Tyne NE1 4ST
Nickname:	The Magpies
Club Colours:	Black and white
Manager:	Kenny Dalglish
Record attendance:	68,386 v Chelsea, 3 September 1930, Division One
Record League victory:	13-0 v Newport County, 5 October 1946, Division Two – Scorers: Shackleton 6, Wayman 4, Milburn 2, Bentley
Record Cup victory:	9-0 v Southport, 1 February 1932, FA Cup Fourth Round – Scorers: Richardson 3, Cape 2, Weaver, Boyd, McMenemy, Lang
Record defeat:	0-9 v Burton Wanderers, 15 April 1895, Division Two
Highest League scorer in a season:	Hughie Gallacher, 36, 1926-27, Division One
Highest League scorer during career:	Jackie Milburn, 178, 1946-57
Most League appearances:	Jim Lawrence, 432, 1904-22

Honours

Premier League Runners-up:	1995-96, 1996-97
Division One Champions:	1904-05, 1908-09, 1926-27, 1992-93
Division Two Champions:	1964-65
Runners-up:	1897-98, 1947-48
FA Cup Winners:	1910, 1924, 1932, 1951, 1952, 1955
Runners-up:	1905, 1906, 1908, 1911, 1974, 1998
Football League Cup Runners-up:	1976
Texaco Cup Winners:	1974, 1975
Anglo-Italian Cup Winners:	1973
European Fairs Cup Winners:	1969

Newcastle United

97/98 Results

August

9	Sheffield Wednesday	H	W	2-1	Asprilla 2, 72
13	Croatia Zagreb (EC Q1-1)	H	W	2-1	Beresford 22, 76
23	Aston Villa	H	W	1-0	Beresford 13
27	Croatia Zagreb (EC Q1-2)	A	D	2-2	Asprilla 44 (pen), Ketsbaia 120

September

13	Wimbledon	H	L	1-3	Barton 32
17	Barcelona (ECL)	H	W	3-2	Asprilla 22 (pen), 30, 48
20	West Ham United	A	W	1-0	Barnes 44
24	Everton	H	W	1-0	Lee 87
27	Chelsea	A	L	0-1	

David Batty.
Phil Cole/Allsport

October

1	Dinamo Kiev (ECL)	A	D	2-2	Beresford 78, Golovko 85 og
4	Tottenham Hotspur	H	W	1-0	Barton 89
15	Hull City (CCC 3)	H	W	2-0	Hamilton 47, Rush 83
18	Leeds United	A	L	1-4	Gillespie 62
22	PSV Eindhoven (ECL)	A	L	0-1	
25	Blackburn Rovers	H	D	1-1	Gillespie 27

November

1	Leicester City	H	D	3-3	Barnes 4 (pen), Tomasson 45, Beresford 90
5	PSV Eindhoven (ECL)	H	L	0-2	
8	Coventry City	A	D	2-2	Barnes 31, Lee 87
18	Derby County (CCC 4)	A	W	1-0	Tomasson 72
22	Southampton	H	W	2-1	Barnes 55, 75
26	Barcelona (ECL)	A	L	0-1	
29	Crystal Palace	A	W	2-1	Ketsbaia 45, Tomasson 63

December

1	Bolton Wanderers	A	L	0-1	
6	Arsenal	H	L	0-1	
10	Dinamo Kiev (ECL)	H	W	2-0	Barnes 10, Pearce 21
13	Barnsley	A	D	2-2	Gillespie 44,49
17	Derby County	H	D	0-0	
21	Manchester United	H	L	0-1	
26	Derby County	A	L	0-1	
28	Liverpool	H	L	1-2	Watson 16

January

3	Everton (FAC 3)	A	W	1-0	Rush 68
7	Liverpool (CCC QF)	H	L	0-2	
10	Sheffield Wednesday	A	L	1-2	Tomasson 20
17	Bolton Wanderers	H	W	2-1	Barnes 6, Ketsbaia 90
20	Liverpool	A	L	0-1	
25	Stevenage (FAC 4)	A	D	1-1	Shearer 3

February

1	Aston Villa	A	W	1-0	Batty 58
4	Stevenage (FAC 4R)	H	W	2-1	Shearer 16, 65
7	West Ham United	H	L	0-1	
14	Tranmere Rovers (FAC 5)	H	W	1-0	Shearer 22
22	Leeds United	H	D	1-1	Ketsbaia 87
28	Everton	A	D	0-0	

March

7	Barnsley (FAC 6)	H	W	3-1	Ketsbaia 16, Speed 27, Batty 90
14	Coventry City	H	D	0-0	
18	Crystal Palace	H	L	1-2	Shearer 77
28	Southampton	A	L	1-2	Lee 46
31	Wimbledon	A	D	0-0	

April

5	Sheffield United (FAC SF)		W	1-0	Shearer 59
11	Arsenal	A	L	1-3	Barton 79
13	Barnsley	H	W	2-1	Andersson 40, Shearer 86
18	Man United	A	D	1-1	Andersson 11
25	Spurs	A	L	0-2	
29	Leicester City	A	D	0-0	

May

2	Chelsea	H	W	3-1	Dabizas 39, Lee 42, Speed 59
10	Blackburn Rovers	A	L	0-1	
16	Arsenal (FAC F)		L	0-2	

Temur Ketsbaia.
Stu Forster/Allsport

Newcastle United

Squad

GOALKEEPERS
SHAY GIVEN
LIONEL PEREZ

DEFENDERS
WARREN BARTON   PHILIPPE ALBERT   ALESSANDRO PISTONE
NIKOS DABIZAS   ANDREW GRIFFIN   STEVE HOWEY   STUART PEARCE
STEVE WATSON   CARL SERRANT   DES HAMILTON
AARON HUGHES

MIDFIELDERS
KEITH GILLESPIE   ROB LEE   DAVID BATTY   JOHN BARNES
JAMES CRAWFORD   TEMUR KETSBAIA   GARY SPEED

STRIKERS
BJARNI GUDJONSSON   ALAN SHEARER   ANDREAS ANDERSSON
IAN RUSH   STEPHANE GUIVARC'H

Philippe Albert
DOB: 10/8/67, Bouillion, Belgium
Signed: Anderlecht, (£2.65 million)
August 1994
League Debut: 21/8/94

Andreas Andersson
DOB: 15/3/74, Sweden
Signed: AC Milan, January 1998
League Debut: 17/1/98

John Barnes
DOB: 7/11/63, Jamaica
Signed: Liverpool, (free) August
1997
League Debut: 13/9/97

Warren Barton
DOB: 19/3/69, London
Signed: Wimbledon, (£4.5 million)
June 1995
League Debut: 19/8/95

David Batty
DOB: 2/12/68, Leeds
Signed: Blackburn Rovers,
(£3.75 million) March 1996
League Debut: 4/3/96

Nikos Dabizas
DOB: 3/8/73, Greece
Signed: Olympiakos, 1998
League Debut: 14/3/98

Keith Gillespie
DOB: 18/2/95, Larne, N Ireland
Signed: Manchester United, (£1
million) January 1995
League Debut: 21/1/95

Shay Given
DOB: 20/4/76, Lifford, Eire
Signed: Blackburn Rovers, (£1.5
million) June 1997
League Debut: 9/8/97

Bjarni Gudjonsson
DOB: 26/2/79, Iceland
Signed: IA Arkanes, (£500,000)
July 1997
League Debut: TBA

Steve Howey
DOB: 26/10/71, Sunderland
Signed: Trainee, December 1989
League Debut: 13/5/89

Temur Ketsbaia
DOB: 18/3/68, Georgia
Signed: AEK Athens, (free)
July 1997
League Debut: 9/8/97

Rob Lee
DOB: 1/2/66, London
Signed: Charlton Athletic,
(£700,000) September 1992
League Debut: 19/9/92

Stuart Pearce
DOB: 24/4/62
Signed: Nottinham Forest, (free)
July 1997
League Debut: 9/8/97

Lionel Perez
DOB: 24/4/67, Bagnols Creze,
France
Signed: Sunderland, (free)
May 1998
League Debut: TBA

Alessandro Pistone
DOB: 27/7/75, Italy
Signed: Inter Milan, (£5 million)
July 1997
League Debut: 9/8/97

Ian Rush
DOB: 20/10/61, St Asaph,
Wales
Signed: Leeds United, (free)
August 1997
League Debut: 23/8/97

Alan Shearer
DOB: 13/8/70, Newcastle
Signed: Blackburn Rovers,
(£15 million) July 1996
League Debut: 17/8/96

Gary Speed
DOB: 8/9/69, Mancot, Wales
Signed: Everton, (£6 million)
January 1998
League Debut: 7/2/98

Steve Watson
DOB: 1/4/74, North Shields
Signed: Trainee, April 1991
League Debut: 10/11/90

1998-99 Premier League Fixtures

	Home	Away
Arsenal	27 Feb	3 Oct
Aston Villa	30 Jan	9 Sep
Blackburn Rovers	16 May	12 Dec
Charlton Athletic	15 Aug	16 Jan
Chelsea	9 Jan	22 Aug
Coventry City	13 Feb	19 Sep
Derby County	17 Oct	3 Apr
Everton	17 Apr	21 Nov
Leeds United	26 Dec	6 Feb
Leicester City	19 Dec	8 May

	Home	Away
Liverpool	29 Aug	28 Dec
Manchester United	13 Mar	7 Nov
Middlesbrough	1 May	5 Dec
Nottingham Forest	26 Sep	6 Mar
Sheffield Wednesday	14 Nov	10 Apr
Southampton	12 Sep	20 Feb
Tottenham Hotspur	5 Apr	24 Oct
West Ham United	31 Oct	20 Mar
Wimbledon	28 Nov	24 Apr

Transfers In: Stephane Guivarc'h (Auxerre £3.5m), Laurent Charvet (Cannes £750,000), Yorgos Yoryadis Panathinaikos £420,000), Gary Brady (Spurs free), Lionel Perez (Sunderland free), Ian Rush.

Tranfers Out: Jon Dahl Tomasson (Feyenoord £2m), Shaka Hislop free (West Ham free), Darren Peacock (Blackburn free), Ian Rush (Wrexham free).

Left: John Barnes, Gary Prior/ Allsport

Below: Team photo. Clive Brunskill/ Allsport

Newcastle United

Tottenham Hotspur

Above: *Darren Anderton.*
Mark Thompson/Allsport

Right: *Sol Campbell.*
Ben Radford/Allsport

'Well at least we didn't lose to Arsenal,' said one Spurs fan having been asked about the 1997-98 season, when a new manager, the return of Klinsman, the silky skills of Ginola and a team sheet that included Sol Campbell, Les Ferdinand, Ruel Fox, Darren Anderton and Chris Armstrong only just kept the team away from relegation. True, the injury list was long and, in the case of Les Ferdinand and Darren Anderton, long-term; and, in spite of Campbell, the defence was a big problem, with 56 goals conceded—but many would question whether Christian Gross really settled down during the season and would point to his relationship with Jürgen Klinsmann as a source of dressing-room problems.

Whatever was going on behind the scenes, on the pitch it took an end of season revival to keep Spurs in the Premiership and make up for a run of 12 games from October to December that saw nine losses and 28 goals against. One loss in the last nine games, eight goals for Klinsmann in that period, the return to fitness of Darren Anderton, whose performances in France '98 showed how much Spurs had missed him, and the prospects for 1998-99 look better than they did at Christmas 1997.

The turning point was probably the 3–3 draw with Liverpool that saw Klinsmann, Ginola and Vega on the scoresheet. Fine wins against Newcastle (2–0 at home) and Wimbledon (6–2 away from home with four from Klinsmann), and a 1–1 draw with Southampton gave seven points in the last three games and that was enough for safety.

There's a long way to go before they can match the great Spurs teams of the past: the Double winners, powered by Dave Mackay and featuring the tireless Bobby Smith up front and the guile of Danny Blanchflower in midfield. Arthur Rowe's 'push and run' side, which won promotion in 1949, the Championship in 1950 and came close the following season, also earned a place in football folklore, while prewar names like Jimmy Seed and Eugene 'Taffy' O'Callaghan stand alongside more recent legends such as Chivers, Gilzean, Perryman and Hoddle as examples of Spurs' illustrious footballing traditions.

Management-wise, no-one has ever eclipsed Rowe and Nicholson. Terry Venables might have, had he not fallen out with owner Alan Sugar, while Gerry Francis, of whom much was expected, was succeeded in 1997 by Swiss national coach Christian Gross. His functional tactics saved the club from the drop in 1997-98, but doubts remained as to his future. For Spurs, it's never been enough to win—they have to win in style.

Season at a Glance

1997-98 Final Position:	14th, Premiership
Top League Goalscorers:	Klinsmann: 9, Ginola: 6, Armstrong: 5, Ferdinand: 5
Highest League win:	6-2 v Wimbledon (A), 2 May 1998
Worst League Defeat:	1-6 Chelsea (H), 6 December 1997
Highest Attendance:	35,995 v Southampton, 10 May 1998
Lowest Attendance:	25,097 v Sheffield Wed, 19 October 1997

PREMIER LEAGUE FOOTBALL

Tottenham Hotspur

Managers

Peter McWilliam	1913-27
Billy Minter	1927-29
Percy Smith	1930-35
Jack Tresadern	1935-38
Peter McWilliam	1938-42
Joe Hulme	1946-49
Arthur Rowe	1949-55
Jimmy Anderson	1955-58
Bill Nicholson	1958-74
Terry Neill	1974-76
Keith Burkinshaw	1976-84
Peter Shreeves	1984-86
David Pleat	1986-87
Terry Venables	1987-91
Peter Shreeves	1991-92
Doug Livermore	1992-93
Ossie Ardiles	1993-94
Gerry Francis	1994-97
Christian Gross	1997-

Above: *Manager Christian Gross.*
Rosss Kinnaird/Allsport

Right: *Les Ferdinand.*
Shaun Botterill/Allsport

Honours

Division One Champions:	1950-51, 1960-61 (Double)
Runners-up:	1921-22, 1951-52, 1956-57, 1962-63
Division Two Champions:	1919-20, 1949-50
Runners-up:	1908-09, 1932-33
FA Cup Winners:	1901, 1921, 1961 (Double), 1962, 1967, 1981, 1982, 1991
Runners-up:	1987
Football League Cup Winners:	1971, 1973
Runners-up:	1982
European Cup Winners' Cup Winners:	1963
Runners-up:	1982
UEFA Cup Winners:	1972, 1984
Runners-up:	1974

Club Details

Year formed:	1882
Ground:	White Hart Lane, Tottenham, London
Nickname:	Spurs
Club Colours:	White and navy blue
Manager:	Christian Gross
Record attendance:	75,038 v Sunderland, 5 March 1938, FA Cup Sixth Round
Record League victory:	9-0 v Bristol Rovers, 22 October 1977, Division Two – Scorers: Lee 4, Morris 3, Hoddle, Taylor
Record Cup victory:	13-2 v Crewe Alexandra, 3 February 1960, FA Cup Fourth Round replay – Scorers: Allen 5, Smith 4, Jones 3 (1 pen), Harmer
Record defeat:	0-7 v Liverpool, 2 September 1978, Division One
Highest League scorer in a season:	Jimmy Greaves, 37, 1962-63, Division One
Highest League scorer during career:	Jimmy Greaves, 220, 1961-70
Most League appearances:	Steve Perryman, 655, 1969-86

Tottenham Hotspur

97/98 Results

August

10	Manchester United	H	L	0-2
13	West Ham United	A	L	1-2	Ferdinand 83
23	Derby County	H	W	1-0	Calderwood 45
27	Aston Villa	H	W	3-2	Ferdinand 6, 66, Fox 77
30	Arsenal	A	D	0-0

September

13	Leicester City	A	L	0-3
17	Carlisle United (CCC 2-1)	H	W	3-2	Fenn 1, Fox 73, Mahorn 78
20	Blackburn Rovers	H	D	0-0
23	Bolton Wanderers	A	D	1-1	Armstrong 71
27	Wimbledon	H	D	0-0
30	Carlisle United (CCC 2-2)	A	W	2-0	Ginola 43 (pen), Armstrong 51

Ramon Vega.
David Cannon/Allsport

October

4	Newcastle	A	L	0-1
15	Derby County (CCC 3)	H	L	1-2	Ginola 22
19	Sheffield Wed	H	W	3-2	Dominguez 6, Armstrong 40, Ginola 45
25	Southampton	A	L	2-3	Dominguez 42, Ginola 65

November

1	Leeds United	H	L	0-1
8	Liverpool	A	L	0-4
24	Crystal Palace	H	L	0-1
29	Everton	A	W	2-0	Vega 72, Ginola 76

December

6	Chelsea	H	L	1-6	Vega 43
13	Coventry City	A	L	0-4
20	Barnsley	H	W	3-0	Nielsen 6, Ginola 12, 18
26	Aston Villa	A	L	1-4	Calderwood 59
28	Arsenal	H	D	1-1	Nielsen 28

January

5	Fulham (FAC 3)	H	W	3-1	Clemence 20, Calderwood 28, Taylor 61 og
10	Manchester United	A	L	0-2	
17	West Ham United	H	W	1-0	Klinsmann 7
24	Barnsley (FAC 4)	H	D	1-1	Campbell 30
31	Derby County	A	L	1-2	Fox 46

February

4	Barnsley (FAC 4R)	A	L	1-3	Ginola 72
7	Blackburn Rovers	A	W	3-0	Berti 37, Armstrong 89, Fox 90
14	Leicester City	H	D	1-1	Calderwood 51
21	Sheffield Wed	A	L	0-1	

March

1	Bolton Wanderers	H	W	1-0	Nielsen 45
4	Leeds United	A	L	0-1	
14	Liverpool	H	D	3-3	Klinsmann 13, Ginola 49, Vega 80
28	Crystal Palace	A	W	3-1	Berti 55, Armstrong 72, Klinsmann 77

April

4	Everton	H	D	1-1	Armstrong 74
11	Chelsea	A	L	0-2	
13	Coventry City	H	D	1-1	Berti 68
18	Barnsley	A	D	1-1	Calderwood 47
25	Newcastle United	H	W	2-0	Klinsmann 31, Ferdinand 73

May

2	Wimbledon	A	W	6-2	Ferdinand 18, Klinsmann 41, 54, 58, 60, Saib 79
10	Southampton	H	D	1-1	Klinsmann 27

David Ginola.
Ben Radford/Allsport

PREMIER LEAGUE FOOTBALL

Tottenham Hotspur

Squad

GOALKEEPERS
IAN WALKER
ESPEN BAARDSEN
FRODE GRODAS

DEFENDERS
JOHN SCALES COLIN CALDERWOOD SOL CAMPBELL FRANCIS BENALI
RAMON VEGA GARY MABBUTT JUSTIN EDINBURGH LEE TODD

MIDFIELDERS
DARREN ANDERTON NICOLA BERTI MOUSSA SAIB DAVID GINOLA
STEPHEN CLEMENCE STEVE CARR JOSE DOMINGUEZ RUEL FOX
ALLAN NIELSEN ANDY SINTON

STRIKERS
CHRIS ARMSTRONG LES FERDINAND STEFFEN IVERSEN
RORY ALLEN PAUL MAHORN

Darren Anderton
DOB: 3/3/72, Southampton
Signed: Portsmouth,
(£1.75 million) June 1992
League Debut: 15/8/92

Chris Armstrong
DOB: 19/6/71, Newcastle
Signed: Crystal Palace,
(£4.5 million) June 1995
League Debut: 19/8/95

Espen Baardsen
DOB: 7/12/77, San Rafael, USA
San Francisco All Blacks (free),
July 1996
League Debut: 3/5/97

Nicola Berti
DOB: 14/4/67, Salsonaggiore, Italy
Signed: Inter Milan, (free) January 1998
League Debut: 10/1/98

Colin Calderwood
DOB: 20/1/65, Stranraer
Signed: Swindon Town,
(£1.25 million) July 1993
League Debut: 14/8/93

Sol Campbell
DOB: 18/9/74, London
Signed: Trainee, September 1992
League Debut: 5/12/92

Steve Carr
DOB: 29/8/76, Dublin
Signed: Trainee, August 1993
League Debut: 26/9/93

Stephen Clemence
DOB: 31/3/78, Liverpool
Signed: Trainee, 1994
League Debut: 10/8/97

Jose Dominguez
DOB: 16/2/74, Lisbon, Portugal
Signed: Sporting Lisbon,
(£1.6 million) August 1997
League Debut: 23/8/97

Les Ferdinand
DOB:8/12/66, London
Signed: Newcastle United,
(£6 million) July 1997
League Debut: 10/8/97

Ruel Fox
DOB: 14/1/68, Ipswich
Signed: Newcastle United,
(£4.2 million) October 1995
League Debut: 14/10/95

David Ginola
DOB: 25/1/67, Gossin, France
Signed: Newcastle United,
(£2.5 million) July 1997
League Debut: 10/8/97

Frode Grodas
DOB: 24/10/64, Hornindal,
Norway
Signed: Chelsea, (£nominal)
January 1998
League Debut: TBA

Steffen Iversen
DOB: 10/11/76, Oslo, Norway
Signed: Rosenborg,
(£2.7 million) December 1996
League Debut: 7/12/96

Gary Mabbutt
DOB: 23/8/61, Bristol
Signed: Bristol Rovers,
(£105,000), August 1982
League Debut: 28/8/82

Allan Nielsen
DOB: 13/3/71, Esjeberg,
Denmark
Signed: Brondby, (£1.65 million)
July 1996
League Debut: 4/9/96

Moussa Saib
DOB: 6/3/69, Theniet, Algeria
Signed: Valencia, (£2.3 million)
February 1998
League Debut: 1/3/98

John Scales
DOB: 4/7/66, Harrogate
Signed: Liverpool,
(£2.6 million) December
1996
League Debut: 1/12/96

Ramon Vega
DOB: 14/6/71, Olten,
Switzerland
Signed: Cagliari,
(£3.75 million) January 1997
League Debut: 12/1/97
Int'l Apps: Full Swiss

Ian Walker
DOB: 31/10/71, Watford
Signed: Trainee, (Price)
December 1989
League Debut: 10/4/91

	Home	Away		Home	Away
Arsenal	10 Apr	14 Nov	Liverpool	5 Dec	1 May
Aston Villa	13 Mar	7 Nov	Manchester United	12 Dec	16 May
Blackburn Rovers	9 Sep	30 Jan	Middlesbrough	12 Sep	20 Feb
Charlton Athletic	31 Oct	20 Mar	Newcastle United	24 Oct	5 Apr
Chelsea	8 May	19 Dec	Nottingham Forest	21 Nov	17 Apr
Coventry City	6 Feb	26 Dec	Sheffield Wednesday	22 Aug	9 Jan
Derby County	27 Feb	3 Oct	Southampton	13 Feb	19 Sep
Everton	28 Dec	29 Aug	West Ham United	24 Apr	28 Nov
Leeds United	26 Sep	6 Mar	Wimbledon	16 Jan	15 Aug
Leicester City	3 Apr	17 Oct			

Transfers In: Paolo Tramezzani (Piacenza £1.4m),
Tranfers Out: Frode Grodas (Schalke 04 £150,000), Paul Mahorn (Port Vale free), Stuart Nethercott (Millwall free), Gary Mabbutt (free), David Howells (Southampton free), Jurgen Klinsmann (free), Dean Austin (Crystal Palace free)

Left: *Moussa Saib.*
Gary M. Prior/Allsport

Below: *Jürgen Klinsman.*
Mark Thompson/Allsport

Tottenham Hotspur

Wimbledon

Above: *Marcus Gayle.*
Gary Clive Brunskill/Allsport

Right: *Robbie Earle.*
Phil Cole/Allsport

Wimbledon's rise from non-League status to the highest heights of English football is said by some to parallel the American maxim that anyone, no matter how lowly-born, can aspire to become President. Others believe their lack of a ground to call their own, plus the long-ball tactics that saw them power through the divisions, somehow make them unworthy to hold such office. Notwithstanding the purists, Wimbledon have got where they are through their own efforts and, though crowds of 8,000 will always make them a club that must sell to survive, a decade of top-flight football proves they are doing something right.

After a brilliant season in 1996-97, when the prospect of the 'Crazy Gang' in Europe became a real possibility, there were great hopes for the 1997-98 season. In the end, it was business as usual at the other end of the table, with only four points separating the Dons from relegated Bolton—although it has to be said that a disastrous end of season run made their final position look a lot worse than at Christmas. After the dispiriting FA Cup fifth round loss to Wolves, Wimbledon had only one win in the last 13 games, which included a 5–0 drubbing by Champions-elect Arsenal, and a 6–2 loss to another London team, Spurs, themselves battling against relegation. It was the lack of goals that caused the problems. Wimbledon could only manage 34, the Premiership's worst: it is to be hoped that Robby Earle can score a few more like the header he put away for Jamaica in France '98, and that strikers Euell, Cort and Gayle can produce more goals than during 1997-98.

For Wimbledon, however, any season that keeps them in the top flight is a success. Following election to League status in 1977, manager Dave Bassett took the Dons to Division One, and his replacement, Bobby Gould, took them to their highest point to date: the FA Cup Final in 1988, when a penalty save by Dave Beasant—the first time a spot-kick at Wembley had not been converted—plus a goal by Lawrie Sanchez saw the Cup end up at 14,000-capacity Plough Lane. The stars of the team like Beasant, striker John Fashanu and Dennis Wise would move on, but the promotion of former Spurs and Eire full-back Joe Kinnear to manager brought another era of success at the club.

They left Plough Lane to groundshare with Crystal Palace in 1991, but rarely filled their new home. Club owner Sam Hammam, tired of the problems of returning Wimbledon to a purpose-built stadium in its own London borough, even suggested a move to Dublin! It's difficult to see how the team survives financially with supporter levels First Division sides would laugh at, but survive it does and, recently, much of that has been down to a unique dressing room atmosphere, fantastic team spirit, Hammam's business acumen, and one of the best managers in football.

Season at a Glance

1997-98 Final Position:	15th, Premiership
Top League Goalscorers:	Hughes: 5, Ekoku: 4, Euell: 4, Leaburn: 4
Highest League win:	4-1 v Barnsley (H), 23 September 1997
Worst League Defeat:	2-6 v Spurs (H), 2 May 1998
Highest Attendance:	26,309 v Man United, 22 November 1997
Lowest Attendance:	7,976 v Barnsley, 23 September 1997

PREMIER LEAGUE FOOTBALL

Wimbledon

Managers

Batsford	1974-77
Dario Gradi	1978-81
Dave Bassett	1981-87
Bobby Gould	1987-90
Ray Harford	1990-91
Peter Withe	1991-92
Joe Kinnear	1992-

Above: *Manager Joe Kinnear.*
Gary M. Prior/Allsport

Right: *Neil Sullivan.*
Dan Smith/Allsport

Club Details

Year formed:	1889
Ground:	Selhurst Park, South Norwood, London SE25 6PY
Nickname:	The Dons
Club Colours:	Navy blue and gold
Manager:	Joe Kinnear
Record attendance:	30,115 v Manchester United, 9 May 1993, FA Premier League
Record League victory:	6-0 v Newport County, 3 September 1983, Division Three – Scorers: Cork 3 (1 pen), Evans 2, Ketteridge
Record Cup victory:	7-2 v Windsor & Eton, 22 November 1980, FA Cup First Round – Scorers: Hubbick 3, Smith 2, Cunningham, Cork
Record defeat:	0-8 v Everton, 29 August 1978, League Cup Second Round
Highest League scorer in a season:	Alan Cork, 29, 1983-84, Division Three
Highest League scorer during career:	Alan Cork, 145, 1977-92
Most League appearances:	Alan Cork, 430, 1977-92

Honours

Division Three Runners-up:	1983-84
Division Four Champions:	1982-83
FA Cup Winners:	1988
League Group Cup Runners-up:	1982
Amateur Cup Winners:	1963
Runners-up:	1935, 1947

Wimbledon

97/98 Results

August

9	Liverpool	H	D	1-1	Gayle 55
23	Sheffield Wednesday	H	D	1-1	Euell 17
27	Chelsea	H	L	0-2	
30	West Ham United	A	L	1-3	Ekoku 81

September

13	Newcastle United	A	W	3-1	Cort 2, Perry 59, Ekoku 76
16	Millwall (CCC 2-1)	H	W	5-1	Cort 23 (pen), 79, Clarke 44, Euell 56, Castledine 86
20	Crystal Palace	H	L	0-1	
23	Barnsley	H	W	4-1	Cort 49, Earle 65, Hughes 68, Ekoku 84
27	Spurs	A	D	0-0	

Neal Ardley.
Shaun Botterill/Allsport

October

1	Millwall (CCC 2-2)	A	W	4-1	Euell 22, 43, Castledine 47, Gayle 50
4	Blackburn	H	L	0-1	
14	Bolton (CCC 3)	A	L	0-2	
18	Aston Villa	A	W	2-1	Earle 39, Cort 61
22	Derby County	A	D	1-1	Rowett 70 og
25	Leeds United	H	W	1-0	Ardley 29 (pen)

November

1	Coventry City	H	L	1-2	Cort 28
10	Leicester City	A	W	1-0	Gayle 50
22	Man U	H	L	2-5	Ardley 68, M Hughes 70
29	Bolton	A	L	0-1	

December

7	Southampton	H	W	1-0	Earle 18
13	Everton	A	D	0-0	
26	Chelsea	A	D	1-1	Hughes 28
28	West Ham	H	L	1-2	Solbakken 90

January

4	Wrexham (FAC 3)	H	D	0-0	
10	Liverpool	A	L	0-2	
13	Wrexham (FAC 3R)	A	W	3-2	M Hughes 17, 26, Gayle 35
17	Derby County	H	D	0-0	
24	Huddersfield Town (FAC 4)	A	W	1-0	Ardley 62
31	Sheffield Wed'day	A	D	1-1	Hughes 21

February

9	Crystal Palace	A	W	3-0	Leaburn 47, 51, Euell 57
14	Wolves (FAC 5)	H	D	1-1	Euell 14
21	Aston Villa	H	W	2-1	Euell 10, Leaburn 39
25	Wolves (FAC 5R)	A	L	1-2	Jones
28	Barnsley	A	L	1-2	Euell 71

March

11	Arsenal	H	L	0-1	
14	Leicester City	H	W	2-1	Roberts 14, M Hughes 62
28	Manchester United	A	L	0-2	
31	Newcastle United	H	D	0-0	

April

4	Bolton Wanderers	H	D	0-0	
11	Southampton	A	W	1-0	Leaburn 38
13	Everton	H	D	0-0	
18	Arsenal	A	L	0-5	
25	Blackburn Rovers	A	D	0-0	
29	Coventry City	A	D	0-0	

May

| 2 | Tottenham Hotspur | H | L | 2-6 | Fear 21, 30 |
| 10 | Leeds United | A | D | 1-1 | Ekoku 88 |

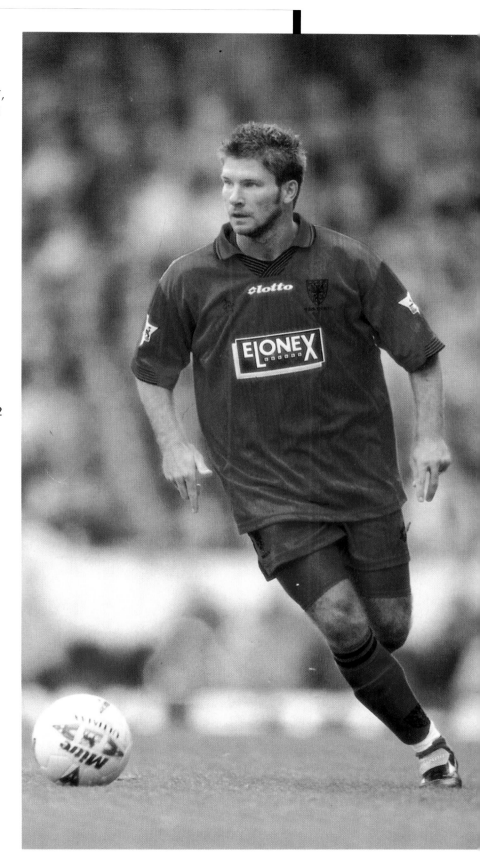

Alan Kimble.
Phil Cole/Allsport

PREMIER LEAGUE FOOTBALL

Squad

GOALKEEPERS
NEIL SULIVAN
PAUL HEALD

DEFENDERS
BEN THATCHER   BRIAN MCALLISTER   ALAN KIMBLE
DUNCAN JUPP   ALAN REEVES   MARCUS HALL
KENNY CUNNINGHAM   CHRIS PERRY   ANDY PEARCE

MIDFIELDERS
ANDY CLARKE   PETER FEAR   ROBBIE EARLE   NEAL ARDLEY
STEWART CASTLEDINE   JASON EUELL   MARK KENNEDY
DAMIAN FRANCIS   MICHAEL HUGHES   STALE SOLBAKKEN
CERI HUGHES

STRIKERS
CARL CORT   EFAN EKOKU   MARCUS GAYLE
CARL LEABURN   JOHN GOODMAN   MICK HARFORD

Neal Ardley
DOB: 1/9/72, Epsom
Signed: Trainee, July 1991
League Debut: 20/4/91

Stewart Castledine
DOB: 22/1/73, London
Signed: Trainee, July 1991
League Debut:

Carl Cort
DOB: 1/11/77, London
Signed: Trainee, Month Year
League Debut: 13/9/97

Kenny Cunningham
DOB: 28/6/71, Dublin
Signed: Milwall, (£1.3 million with
Jon Goodman) November 1994
League Debut: 19/11/94

Robbie Earle
DOB: 27/1/65, Newcastle Under
Lyme
Signed: Port Vale, (£775,000)
July 1991
League Debut: 17/8/91

Efan Ekoku
DOB: 8/6/67, Manchester
Signed: Norwich City, (£900,000)
March 1993
League Debut: 17/10/94

Jason Euell
DOB: 6/2/77, London
Signed:Trainee, June 1995
League Debut: 28/11/95

Peter Fear
DOB: 11/9/73, Sutton
Signed: Trainee, July 1992
League Debut: 10/2/93

Damian Francis
DOB: 18/4/98 , Place ,(Country
if foreign)
Signed: Team/Apprentice, (Price)
Month Year
League Debut: 18/4/98

Marcus Gayle
DOB: 27/9/70, London
Signed: Brentford, (£250,000)
March 1994
League Debut: 26/3/94

Paul Heald
DOB: 20/9/68, Wath on Dearne
Signed: Leyton Orient, (£250,000)
July 1995
League Debut: 19/8/95

Ceri Hughes
DOB: 26/2/71, Pontypridd, Wales
Signed: Luton Town, (£400,000)
July 1997
League Debut: 9/8/97

Duncan Jupp
DOB: 25/1/75
Signed: Fulham, (£200,000)
June 1996
League Debut: 28/12/96

Mark Kennedy
DOB: 6/8/66, Dublin
Signed: Liverpool,
(£1.75 million) March 1988
League Debut: 25/8/98

Alan Kimble
DOB: 6/8/66, Dagenham
Signed: Camnbridge United,
(£175,000) July 1993
League Debut: 14/8/93

Carl Leaburn
DOB: 30/3/69, London
Signed: Charlton Athletic,
(£300,000) January 1998
League Debut: 10/1/98

Brian McAllister
DOB: 30/11/70, Glasgow
Signed: Trainee, March 1989
League Debut: 13/1/90

Chris Perry
DOB: 26/4/75, Carshalton
Signed: Trainee, July 1991
League Debut: 4/4/94

Andy Roberts

DOB: 20/3/74, Dartford
Signed: Crystal Palace
(£1.6 million) March 1998
League Debut: 11/3/98

Neil Sullivan
DOB: 24/2/70, Sutton
Signed: Trainee, July 1988
League Debut: 20/4/91

Ben Thatcher
DOB: 30/11/75, Swindon
Signed: Millwall, (£1.82 million)
1996
League Debut: 17/8/96

	Home	Away		Home	Away
Arsenal	21 Nov	17 Apr	Liverpool	12 Dec	16 May
Aston Villa	20 Feb	12 Sep	Manchester United	3 Apr	17 Oct
Blackburn Rovers	31 Oct	20 Mar	Middlesbrough	24 Oct	5 Apr
Charlton Athletic	26 Dec	6 Feb	Newcastle United	24 Apr	28 Nov
Chelsea	10 Apr	14 Nov	Nottingham Forest	13 Mar	7 Nov
Coventry City	5 Dec	1 May	Sheffield Wednesday	19 Sep	13 Feb
Derby County	9 Jan	22 Aug	Southampton	8 May	19 Dec
Everton	3 Oct	27 Feb	Tottenham Hotspur	15 Aug	16 Jan
Leeds United	29 Aug	28 dec	West Ham United	30 Jan	9 Sep
Leicester City	6 Mar	26 Sep			

Transfers In: None
Tranfers Out: None

Left: Carl Leaburn. Phil Cole/Allsport

Below: Selhurst Park, home of Wimbledon. Ross Kinnaird/ Allsport

PREMIER LEAGUE FOOTBALL

Wimbledon

Sheffield Wednesday

Above: *Benito Carbone*
Ross Kinnaird/Allsport

Right: *Dejan Stefanovic*
Mark Thompson/Allsport

Founded in 1867, Sheffield Wednesday have a proud history which includes victories in all the major domestic competitions, but for many years the trophy cabinet was empty and the club failed to fulfil its potential. Indeed, Wednesday's triumph in the 1991 League Cup Final was their first major prize, discounting three Second Division Championships, since 1935.

At no stage in the 1997-98 season, however, did it look as if Wednesday would need to make space in the cabinet for more silverware. In spite of four Carbone goals in August, losses to Newcastle, Leeds and Blackburn set the tone for the season.

It got worse. In September they lost in the Coca-Cola Cup to Grimsby, going down 3–4 over the two legs. In the Premiership there would be 18 losses in total, more than any club except Barnsley and Palace, and 67 goals against.

And yet it was not all doom and gloom. Under the mercurial hand of Ron Atkinson, the side stayed in the Premiership and more than that: it played a significant role in deciding the fortunes of the championship when on 7 March 1998, at a crucial time in the run-in to the title, the Owls won back the gratitude of the Highbury fans by defeating Manchester United 2–0. 'Won back'? Well Wednesday had more than displeased the Gunners by taking three points off them before Christmas in a 2–0 home victory secured thanks to strikes by Booth and Whittingham!

Wednesday started their League career in Division One in 1892, and within 15 years had achieved two FA Cup victories and two League titles. By the mid-1970s, however, they were at the nadir of the club's fortunes relegated to the Third Division in 1975.

The managerial skills of first Jack Charlton and then Howard Wilkinson guided Wednesday back to the top flight by 1985, although they were to spend one further season in Division Two in 1990-91. Under Ron Atkinson, Wednesday came straight back up and completed an impressive season by triumphing over Atkinson's former charges Manchester United in the League Cup Final. But the following season was to bring frustration as they finished third in the last of the pre-Premiership First Division campaigns and lost to Arsenal in both domestic Cup Finals under the leadership of Trevor Francis.

Mid-1990s Wednesday flattered to deceive, and after Ron Atkinson was recruited as a short-term replacement for David Pleat in late 1997 to successfully stave off relegation from the Premiership, they took their time appointing a supremo to lead them into the new millennium, in the end choosing Barnsley's Danny Wilson.

Season at a Glance

1997-98 Final Position:	16th, Premiership
Top League Goalscorers:	Di Canio: 12, Carbone: 9, Booth: 7
Highest League win:	5-0 v Bolton (H), 8 November 1997
Worst League Defeat:	2-7 v Blackburn (A), 25 August 1997
Highest Attendance:	39,427 v Man United, 7 March 1998
Lowest Attendance:	21,087 v Coventry City, 20 September 1997

PREMIER LEAGUE FOOTBALL

Sheffield Wednesday

Managers

Rob Brown	1920-33
Billy Walker	1933-37
Jimmy McMullan	1937-42
Eric Taylor	1942-58
Harry Catterick	1958-61
Vic Buckingham	1961-64
Alan Brown	1964-68
Jack Marshall	1968-69
Danny Williams	1969-71
Derek Dooley	1971-73
Steve Burtenshaw	1974-75
Len Ashurst	1975-77
Jack Charlton	1977-83
Howard Wilkinson	1983-88
Peter Eustace	1988-89
Ron Atkinson	1989-91
Trevor Francis	1991-95
David Pleat	1995-97
Ron Atkinson	1997-98
Danny Wilson	1998-

Above: *Manager Danny Wilson.*
Stu Forster/Allsport

Right: *Paolo di Canio.*
David Rawcliffe/Allsport

Honours

Division One Champions:	1902-03, 1903-04, 1928-29, 1929-30
Runners-up:	1960-61
Division Two Champions:	1899-1900, 1925-26, 1951-52, 1955-56, 1958-59
Runners-up:	1949-50, 1983-84
FA Cup Winners:	1896, 1907, 1935
Runners-up:	1890, 1966, 1993
Football League Cup Winners:	1991
Runners-up:	1993

Club Details

Year formed:	1867
Ground:	Hillsborough, Sheffield S6 1SW
Nickname:	The Owls
Club Colours:	Blue and white
Manager:	TBA
Record attendance:	72, 841 v Manchester City, 17 February 1934,
Record League victory:	9-1 v Birmingham, 13 December 1930, Division One – Scorers: Hooper 3, Seed 2, Ball 2, Burgess, Rimmer
Record Cup victory:	12-0 v Halliwell, 17 January 1891, FA Cup First Round – Scorers: Woolhouse 5, Cawley 2, Mumford 2, H Brandon, B Brandon, Ingram
Record defeat:	0-10 v Aston Villa, 5 October 1912, Division One
Highest League scorer in a season:	Derek Dooley, 46, 1951-52, Division Two
Highest League scorer during career:	Andy Wilson, 199, 1900-20
Most League appearances:	Andy Wilson, 502, 1900-20

Sheffield Wednesday

97/98 Results

August
9	Newcastle United	A	L	1-2	Carbone 8
13	Leeds United	H	L	1-3	Hyde 70
23	Wimbledon	A	D	1-1	Di Canio 75
25	Blackburn Rovers	A	L	2-7	Carbone 8, 47
30	Leicester City	H	W	1-0	Carbone 56 (pen)

September
13	Liverpool	A	L	1-2	Collins 80
17	Grimsby Town (CCC 2-1)	A	L	0-2	
20	Coventry City	H	D	0-0	
24	Derby County	H	L	2-5	Di Canio 5, Carbone 12 (pen)
27	Aston Villa	A	D	2-2	Collins 26, Whittingham 42

Graham Hyde.
Stu Forster/Allsport

October
1	Grimsby (CCC 2-2)	H	W	3-2	Davison 16 og, Di Canio 64, 88
4	Everton	H	W	3-1	Carbone 78, 82 (pen), Di Canio 89
19	Spurs	A	L	2-3	Collins 72, Di Canio 85
25	Palace	H	L	1-3	Collins 57

November
1	Man U	A	L	1-6	Whittingham 69
8	Bolton	H	W	5-0	Di Canio 20, Whittingham 26, Booth 29, 33, 44
22	Arsenal	H	W	2-0	Booth 42, Whittingham 86
29	Southampton	A	W	3-2	Atherton 28, Collins 69, Di Canio 84

December
8	Barnsley	H	W	2-1	Stefanovic 19, Di Canio 88
13	West Ham	A	L	0-1	
20	Chelsea	H	L	1-4	Pembridge 71
26	Blackburn	H	D	0-0	
28	Leicester City	A	D	1-1	Booth 85

January

3	Watford (FAC 3)	A	D	1-1	Alexandersson 64
10	Newcastle United	H	W	2-1	Di Canio 1,Newsome 51
14	Watford (FAC 3R)	H	W	0-0 (Won 5-3 on penalties)	
17	Leeds United	A	W	2-1	Newsome 51, Booth 83
26	Blackburn Rovers (FAC 4)	H	L	0-3	
31	Wimbledon	H	D	1-1	Pembridge 14

February

7	Coventry City	A	L	0-1	
14	Liverpool	H	D	3-3	Carbone 7, Di Canio 63, Hinchcliffe 69
21	Tottenham Hotspur	H	W	1-0	Di Canio 33
28	Derby County	A	L	0-3	

March

7	Manchester United	H	W	2-0	Atherton 26, Di Canio 88
14	Bolton Wanderers	A	L	2-3	Booth 26, Atherton 59
28	Arsenal	A	L	0-1	

April

4	Southampton	H	W	1-0	Carbone 78
11	Barnsley	A	L	1-2	Stefanovic 86
13	West Ham United	H	D	1-1	Magilton 59
19	Chelsea	A	L	0-1	
25	Everton	A	W	3-1	Pembridge 6, 41, Di Canio 90

May

2	Aston Villa	H	L	1-3	Sanetti 89
10	Crystal Palace	A	L	0-1	

Andy Booth.
David Rawcliffe/Allsport

PREMIER LEAGUE FOOTBALL

Sheffield Wednesday

Squad

GOALKEEPERS
KEVIN PRESSMAN
MATT CLARKE
BRUCE GROBBELAAR

DEFENDERS
EARL BARRETT   DES WALKER   JON NEWSOME   ANDY HINCHCLIFFE
IAN NOLAN   GOCE SEDLOSKI   DEJAN STEFANOVIC
STEVE NICOL   LEE BRISCO

MIDFIELDERS
BENITO CARBONE   PETER ATHERTON   MARK PEMBRIDGE   PETTER RUDI
GRAHAM HYDE   JIM MAGILTON   NICLAS ANDERSSON
SCOT OAKES   EMERSON THOME   RYAN JONES

STRIKERS
ANDY BOOTH   GUY WHITTINGHAM   PAOLO DI CANIO
RICHIE HUMPHREYS

Peter Atherton
DOB: 6/4/70, Orrell
Signed: Coventry City, (£800,000)
June 1994
League Debut: 20/8/94

Earl Barrett
DOB: 28/4/67, Rochdale
Signed: Everton, (free) February
1998
League Debut: 28/2/98

Andy Booth
DOB: 6/12/73, Huddersfield
Signed: Huddersfield Town,
(£2.7 million) July 1996
League Debut: 17/8/96

Benito Carbone
DOB: 14/8/71, Bagnara Calabra
Signed: Inter Milan, (£4 million)
1996
League Debut: 19/10/96

Matt Clarke
DOB: 3/11/73, Sheffield
Signed: Rotherham United,
(£325,000) July 1996
League Debut: 11/5/97

Paolo Di Canio
DOB: 9/7/68, Rome, Italy
Signed: Glasgow Celtic,
(£4.5 million) July 1997
League Debut: 9/8/97

Andy Hinchcliffe
DOB: 5/2/69, Manchester
Signed: Everton, (£3 million)
January 1998
League Debut: 31/1/98

Richie Humphreys
DOB: 30/11/77, Sheffield
Signed: Trainee
League Debut: 9/9/95

Graham Hyde
DOB: 10/11/70, Doncaster
Signed: Trainee, May 1988
League Debut: 14/9/91

Jim Magilton
DOB: 6/5/69, Belfast, N Ireland
Signed: Southampton,
(£1.6 million) September 1997
League Debut: 13/9/97

Jon Newsome
DOB: 6/9/70, Sheffield
Signed: Trainee, July 1989
League Debut: 9/9/89

Ian Nolan
DOB: 9/7/70, Liverpool
Signed: Tranmere Rovers,
(£1.5 million) August 1994
League Debut: 20/8/94

Mark Pembridge
DOB: 29/11/70, Merthyr Tydfil
Signed: Derby County,
(£900,000) July 1995
League Debut: 19/9/95

Kevin Pressman
DOB: 6/11/67, Fareham
Signed: Apprentice, November
1985
League Debut: 5/9/87

Petter Rudi
DOB: 17/9/73, Norway
Signed: Molde, (£800,000)
October 1997
League Debut: 19/10/97

Goce Sedloski
DOB: 10/4/74, Macedonia
Signed: Hajduk Split, (£750,000)
February 1998
League Debut: 14/3/98

Dejan Stefanovic
DOB: 28/10/74, Yugoslavia
Signed: Red Star Belgrade,
(£4.5 million) 1995
League Debut: 26/12/95

Emerson Thome
DOB: unknown, Brazil
Signed: Benfica, (free) March
1998
League Debut: 11/4/98

Des Walker
DOB: 26/11/65, London
Signed: Sampdoria,
(£2.7 million) July 1993
League Debut: 14/8/93

Guy Whittingham
DOB: 10/11/64, Evesham
Signed: Aston Villa,
(£700,000) December 1994
League Debut: 3/12/94

1998-99 Premier League Fixtures

	Home	Away		Home	Away
Arsenal	26 Sep	6 Mar	Liverpool	8 May	19 Dec
Aston Villa	29 Aug	28 Dec	Manchester United	21 Nov	17 Apr
Blackburn Rovers	12 Sep	20 Feb	Middlesbrough	27 Feb	3 Oct
Charlton Athletic	12 Dec	16 May	Newcastle United	10 Apr	14 Nov
Chelsea	24 Apr	28 Nov	Nottingham Forest	5 Dec	1 May
Coventry City	3 Apr	17 Oct	Southampton	31 Oct	20 Mar
Derby County	30 Jan	9 Sep	Tottenham Hotspur	9 Jan	22 Aug
Everton	24 Oct	5 Apr	West Ham United	15 Aug	16 Jan
Leeds United	13 Mar	7 Nov	Wimbledon	13 Feb	19 Sep
Leicester City	26 Dec	6 Feb			

Left: *Andy Hinchcliffe.*
Stu Forster/Allsport

Below: *Hillsborough, home of Sheffield Wednesday.*

Transfers In: Wim Jonk (PSV Eindhoven £2.5m)
Tranfers Out: Mark Pembridge (Benfica free)

PREMIER LEAGUE FOOTBALL

Sheffield Wednesday

Everton

Above: *Danny Cadamanteri.* Clive Brunskill/Allsport

Right: *Duncan Ferguson.* Alex Livesey/Allsport

'The luckiest club in England,' was how it was reported when a nail-biting season ended with joy for Howard Kendall and a reprieve on goal difference from relegation for the Toffees. Merseyside's senior club were among the League's founder members in 1888, having developed from a church team, St Domingo's, during the preceding decade. Despite leaving their original ground, Anfield, after a row with the landlord John Houlding (who promptly formed Liverpool FC), they built Goodison Park in record time, and the stadium with its multi-tiered stands remains a masterpiece today.

The teams that have attempted to fill it have varied considerably in their success. Yet the club has maintained a reputation for playing attractive, entertaining football which, though it hasn't of late brought as many trophies as has that of the team across Stanley Park, has secured several titles. Premiership silverware was definitely not on the cards in 1997-98, and at first sight, there seemed little good to come out of a season that saw only nine wins in the Premiership. But examine those wins more closely and see just how narrow the difference between league success and failure. The team that lacked the consistency to do more than stave off relegation shared four goals with Champions Arsenal; beat Liverpool 2–0 at home and drew 1–1 away; defeated fourth-placed Chelsea 3–1 in January and took three points from both fifth-placed Leeds United (2–0) and sixth-placed Blackburn Rovers (1–0)—so four of the nine wins were against top opposition. With this sort of ability canny Walter Smith, the new manager, at least has something to build on to emulate the glories of Everton's past.

Two League wins in 1891 and 1915, divided by an FA Cup triumph in 1906, were followed by the 1927-28 Championship and another, a decade later, in 1939. Pools millionaire John Moores took on the chairmanship and appointed Harry Catterick manager. The League came in 1963 and 1970, the Cup in 1966, but the 1970s were relatively barren years as Bill Shankly and then Bob Paisley led their Red rivals to trophies a-plenty.

Former midfielder Howard Kendall restored hope after his 1981 appointment, securing two Championships and the FA Cup in four seasons as well as the European Cup Winners' Cup, with names like Gray, Ratcliffe, Sharpe and Southall. A rapid turnover at the helm after Kendall left for Spain saw fortunes slump, apart from Joe Royale's 1995 team's FA Cup victory. But supporter dissent and boardroom indecision cast double gloom over Everton's prospects and Kendall returned and departed by mutual consent as 1998-99 loomed. Enter ex-Rangers manager Walter Smith and a new broom.

Season at a Glance

1997-98 Final Position:	17th in the Premiership
Top League Goalscorers:	Ferguson: 11, Speed: 7, Madar: 6
Highest League win:	4-2 v Barnsley (H), 20 September 1997
Worst League Defeat:	0-4 v Arsenal (A), 3 May 1998
Highest Attendance:	40,112 v Liverpool, 18 October 1997
Lowest Attendance:	28,533 v Wimbledon, 13 December 1997

Everton

Managers

Theo Kelly	1939-48
Cliff Britton	1948-56
Ian Buchan	1956-58
John Carey	1958-61
Harry Catterick	1961-73
Billy Bingham	1973-77
Gordon Lee	1977-81
Howard Kendall	1981-87
Colin Harvey	1987-90
Howard Kendall	1990-93
Mike Walker	1994
Joe Royle	1994-97
Howard Kendall	1997-98
Walter Smith	1998-

Above: *Manager Walter Smith.*
David Rawcliffe/Allsport

Right: *Slaven Bilic.*
Shaun Botterill/Allsport

Honours

Division One Champions:	1890-91, 1914-15, 1927-28, 1931-32, 1938-39, 1962-63, 1969-70, 1984-85, 1986-87
Runners-up:	1889-90, 1894-95, 1901-02, 1904-05,
Division Two Champions:	1930-31
Runners-up:	1953-54
FA Cup Winners:	1906, 1933, 1966, 1984, 1995
Runners-up:	1893, 1897, 1907, 1968, 1985, 1986, 1989
Football League Cup Runners-up:	1977, 1984
League Super Cup Runners-up:	1986
Simod Cup Runners-up:	1989
Zenith Data System Cup Runners-up:	1991
European Cup Winners' Cup Winners:	1985

Club Details

Year formed:	1878
Ground:	Goodison Park, Liverpool L4 4EL
Nickname:	The Toffees
Club Colours:	Blue and white
Manager:	Walter Smith
Record attendance:	78,299 v Liverpool, 18 September 1948, Division One
Record League victory:	9-1 v Manchester City, 3 September 1906, Division One – Scorers: Young 4, Settle 2, Taylor, Abbott, Bolton; v Plymouth Argyle, 27 December 1930, Division Two – Scorers: Dean 4, Stein 4, Johnson
Record Cup victory:	11-2 v Derby County, 18 January 1890, FA Cup First Round – Scorers: Brady 3, Geary 3, Millward 3, Doyle, Holt, League Cup Second Round
Record defeat:	4-10 v Tottenham Hotspur, 11 October 1958, Division One
Highest League scorer in a season:	Dixie Dean, 60, 1927-28, Division One
Highest League scorer during career:	Dixie Dean, 349, 1925-37
Most League appearances:	Neville Southall, 578, 1981-98

Everton

97/98 Results

August

9	Crystal Palace	H	L	1-2	Ferguson 85
23	West Ham United	H	W	2-1	Speed 67, Stuart 83
27	Manchester United	H	L	0-2	

September

1	Bolton Wanderers	A	D	0-0	
13	Derby County	A	L	1-3	Stuart 28
16	Scunthorpe United (CCC 2-1)	A	W	1-0	Farrelly 36
20	Barnsley	H	W	4-2	Speed 12, 77 (pen), Cadamarteri 42, Oster 84
24	Newcastle United	A	L	0-1	
27	Arsenal	H	D	2-2	Ball 49, Cadamarteri 56

Nick Barmby.
Clive Brunskill/Allsport

October

1	Scunthorpe (CCC 2-2)	H	W	5-0	Stuart 11, Oster 23,67, Barmby 66, Cadamarteri 69
4	Sheffield	A	L	1-3	Cadamarteri 84
15	Coventry City (CCC 3)	A	L	1-4	Barmby 16
18	Liverpool	H	W	2-0	Ruddock 45 og, Cadamarteri 75
25	Coventry City	A	D	0-0	

November

2	Southampton	H	L	0-2	
8	Blackburn	A	L	2-3	Speed 7, Ferguson 55
22	Aston Villa	A	L	1-2	Speed 12 (pen)
26	Chelsea	A	L	0-2	
29	Spurs	H	L	0-2	

December

6	Leeds United	A	D	0-0	
13	Wimbledon	H	D	0-0	
20	Leicester City	A	W	1-0	Speed 89 (pen)
26	Man. United	A	L	0-2	
28	Bolton W'drs	H	W	3-2	Ferguson 17, 41, 67

January

3	Newcastle (FAC 3)	H	L	0-1	
10	Crystal Palace	A	W	3-1	Barmby 3, Ferguson 12, Madar 34
18	Chelsea	H	W	3-1	Speed 39, Ferguson 62, Duberry 83 og
31	West Ham	A	D	2-2	Barmby 25, Madar 60

February

7	Barnsley	A	D	2-2	Ferguson 40, Grant 50
14	Derby County	H	L	1-2	Thomsen 85
23	Liverpool	A	D	1-1	Ferguson 58
28	Newcastle United	H	D	0-0	

March

7	Southampton	A	L	1-2	Tiler 89
14	Blackburn	H	W	1-0	Madar 62
28	Aston Villa	H	L	1-4	Madar 38

April

4	Spurs	A	D	1-1	Madar 24
11	Leeds	H	W	2-0	Hutchison 10, Ferguson 38
13	Wimbledon	A	D	0-0	
18	Leicester City	H	D	1-1	Madar 2
25	Shef'd Wed	H	L	1-3	Ferguson 72

May

3	Arsenal	A	L	0-4	
10	Coventry City	H	D	1-1	Farrelly 7

Terry Phelan. Dave Rawcliffe/Allsport

PREMIER LEAGUE FOOTBALL

Everton

Squad

GOALKEEPERS
THOMAS MYHRE
PAUL GERRARD

DEFENDERS
EARL BARRETT   DAVE WATSON   SLAVEN BILIC   CARL TILER
CRAIG SHORT   JOHN O'KANE   TERRY PHELAN
TONY THOMAS   CLAUS THOMSEN   MICHAEL BALL

MIDFIELDERS
TONY GRANT   GARETH FARRELLY   NICK BARMBY   DON HUTCHISON
DANNY WILLIAMSON   JOE PARKINSON   JOHN OSTER
GRAHAM HUGES   MITCH WARD   DANNY CADAMARTERI

STRIKERS
JOHN SPENCER   DUNCAN FERGUSON   MICKAEL MADAR
MICHAEL BRANCH

Michael Ball
DOB: 2/10/79, Liverpool
Signed: Trainee
League Debut: 12/4/97

Nick Barmby
DOB: 11/2/74, Hull
Signed: Middlesbrough,
(£5.75 million) October 1996
League Debut: 4/11/96

Slaven Bilic
DOB: 11/9/68, Croatia
Signed: West Ham United,
(£4.5 million) June 1997
League Debut: 9/8/97

Gareth Farrelly
DOB: 28/8/75, Dublin, Eire
Signed: Aston Villa, (£700,000)
July 1997
League Debut: 9/8/97

Duncan Ferguson
DOB: 27/12/71, Stirling, Scotland
Signed: Glasgow Rangers,
(£4.4 million) December 1994
League Debut: 15/10/94 (on loan)

Paul Gerrard
DOB: 22/1/73, Heywood
Signed: Oldham Athletic,
(£1 million) August 1996
League Debut: 16/11/96

Mickael Madar
DOB: 5/8/68, France
Signed: Deportivo La Coruna,
(free) January 1998
League Debut: 10/1/98

Thomas Myhre
DOB: 16/10/73, Sarpsborg,
Norway
Signed: Viking Stavanger,
(£800,000) November 1997
League Debut: 6/12/97

John O'Kane
DOB: 15/11/74, Nottingham
Signed: Manchester United,
(£500,000) January 1998
League Debut: 31/1/98

John Oster
DOB: 8/12/78, Boston,
Lincolnshire
Signed: Grimsby Town,
(£1.5 million) July 1997
League Debut: 9/8/97

Joe Parkinson
DOB: 11/6/71, Eccles
Signed: Bournemouth, (£250,000)
March 1994
League Debut: 20/8/94

Terry Phelan
DOB: 16/3/67, Manchester
Signed: Chelsea, (£850,000)
December 1996
League Debut: 1/1/97

Craig Short
DOB: 25/6/68, Bridlington
Signed: Derby County,
(£2.7 million) July 1995
League Debut: 17/9/95

John Spencer
DOB: 11/9/70, Glasgow
Signed: Queens Park Rangers,
March 1998 (on loan)
League Debut: 14/3/98 (on loan)

Tony Thomas
DOB: 12/7/71, Liverpool
Signed: Tranmere Rovers,
(£400,000) July 1997
League Debut: 9/8/97

Claus Thomsen
DOB: 31/5/70, Aarhus,
Denmark
Signed: Ipswich Town,
(£900,000) January 1997
League Debut: 19/1/97

Carl Tiler
DOB: 11 February 1970,
Sheffield
Signed: Sheffield United, (With
Ward, £250,000 plus Graham
Stuart) November 1997
League Debut: 29/11/97

Mitch Ward
DOB: 19 June 1971, Sheffield
Signed: Sheffield United, (With
Tiler, £250,000 plus Graham
Stuart) November 1997
League Debut: 26/11/97

Danny Williamson
DOB: 16/10/73, Preston
Signed: West Ham United,
(£1 million plus David
Unsworth) August 1997
League Debut: 23/8/97

1998-99 Premier League Fixtures

	Home	Away		Home	Away
Arsenal	13 Mar	7 Nov	Manchester United	31 Oct	20 Mar
Aston Villa	15 Aug	16 Jan	Middlesbrough	13 Feb	19 Sep
Blackburn Rovers	26 Sep	6 Mar	Newcastle United	21 Nov	17 Apr
Charlton Athletic	24 Apr	28 Nov	Nottingham Forest	30 Jan	9 Sep
Chelsea	5 Dec	1 May	Sheffield Wednesday	5 Apr	24 Oct
Coventry City	10 Apr	14 Nov	Southampton	12 Dec	16 May
Derby County	26 Dec	6 Feb	Tottenham Hotspur	29 Aug	28 Dec
Leeds United	12 Sep	20 Feb	West Ham United	8 May	19 Dec
Leicester City	9 Jan	22 Aug	Wimbledon	27 Feb	3 Oct
Liverpool	17 Oct	3 Apr			

Left: *Earl Barrett.*
Clive Brunskill/
Allsport

Below: *Duncan Ferguson.*
Alex Livesey/
Allsport

Transfers In: Maro Materazzi (Perugia £2.75m), John Collins (Monaco £2.5m), Oliver Dacourt (Strasbourg £3,800,000)
Tranfers Out: None

163

Everton

PREMIER LEAGUE FOOTBALL

*Paul Merson strikes for
goal.*
Shaun Botterill/Allsport

Nottingham Forest

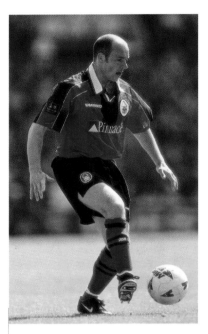

Above: *Steve Stone.*
Clive Brunskill/Allsport

Right: *Pierre Van Hooijdonk.*
Ross Kinnaird/Allsport

If Nottingham Forest fans had a pound for every time they'd heard that their club was 'too good to be relegated' they'd be able to buy Alan Shearer! Nevertheless, it's true that the club has a long-standing reputation for playing entertaining football, but until relatively recently this had never translated itself into trophies. For almost a century, Forest played their football with panache, but it took the inimitable Brian Clough to transform them into a side with the killer instinct.

One of the oldest surviving clubs in the world, Forest were formed in 1865, and joined a newly-enlarged First Division in 1892. There they stayed for most of the period leading up to the First World War, tasting success by winning the FA Cup at their first Final in 1898 but doing little else.

This unremarkable period ended in 1950, not with the eagerly-awaited promotion, but with an unprecedented drop into Division Three (South). Forest stood by manager Billy Walker, and he repaid their faith by rebuilding the side and, in 1957, leading them back to the First Division. A second FA Cup success followed in 1959, and for almost 20 years Forest played in the top flight with modest success. Their best season was 1966-67, when they finished second in the League, and were FA Cup semi-finalists, but a decline followed and the unpopular sale of several star players preceded relegation in 1972.

Brian Clough arrived as manager in 1975, and took the club by the scruff of the neck. He and assistant Peter Taylor steered the club to promotion, their first ever League Championship and two European Cup victories in successive seasons, keeper Peter Shilton, defender Kenny Burns and forward Tony Woodcock all key players in the most successful Forest side yet. Throughout the 1980s, Clough kept Forest there or thereabouts, but the success came to an end with relegation after the first Premiership season.

Clough's less than elegant departure and the exodus of star players didn't, however, prevent an immediate return to the top under Frank Clark. But a yo-yo sequence of relegation and promotion, the latter achieved in 1998 under Dave Bassett, suggested Forest were unlikely to regain their Clough-given status in the face of the new elite. Even their Dutch international top scorer Van Hooijdonk—who put away 29 chances in 1997-98—was available at the right price, Bassett revealed. Following Kevin Campbell's move to Turkey it remains to be seen whether the volatile Dutch star can be kept at the club..

Season at a Glance

1997-98 Final Position:	1st in Division One
Top League Goalscorers:	Van Hooijdonk: 29, Campbell: 23, Cooper: 5
Highest League win:	5-2 v Charlton Athletic (H), 22 November 1997
Worst League Defeat:	2-4 v Charlton Athletic (A), 28 March 1998
Highest Attendance:	29,302 v Reading, 26 April 1998
Lowest Attendance:	16,524 v Norwich City, 15 August 1997

PREMIER LEAGUE FOOTBALL

Nottingham Forest

Managers

Harold Whittingham	1936-39
Billy Walker	1939-60
Andy Beattie	1960-63
John Carey	1963-68
Matt Gillies	1969-72
Dave Mackay	1972-73
Allan Brown	1973-75
Brian Clough	1975-93
Frank Clark	1993-96
Stuart Pearce	1996-97
Dave Bassett	1997-

Above: *Manager Dave Basset.*
Ross Kinnaird/Allsport

Right: *Kevin Campbell.*
Ben Radford/Allsport

Honours

Division One Champions:	1977-78, 1997-98
Runners-up:	1966-67, 1978-79
Division Two Champions:	1906-07, 1921-22
Runners-up:	1956-57
Division Three (South) Champions:	1950-51
FA Cup Winners:	1898, 1959
Runners-up:	1991
Football League Cup Winners:	1978, 1979, 1989, 1990
Runners-up:	1980
Anglo-Scottish Cup Winners:	1977
Simod Cup Winners:	1989
Zenith Data Systems Cup Winners:	1992
European Cup Winners:	1979, 1980
Super Cup Winners:	1980
Runners-up:	1981
World Club Championship Runners-up:	1980

Club Details

Year formed:	1865
Ground:	City Ground, Nottingham NG2 5FJ
Nickname:	The Reds
Club Colours:	Red, black and white
Manager:	Dave Bassett
Record attendance:	49,946 v Manchester United, 28 October 1967,
Record League victory:	2-0 v Leicester Fosse, 12 April 1909, Division One – Scorers: Hooper 3, West 3, Spouncer 3 (1 pen), Morris 2, Hughes
Record Cup victory:	14-0 v Clapton, 17 January 1891, FA Cup First Round – Scorers: Higgins 5, Lindley 4, McCallum 2, Shaw 2, Tich Smith
Record defeat:	1-9 v Blackburn Rovers, 10 April 1937, Division Two
Highest League scorer in a season:	Wally Ardron, 36, 1950-51, Division Three (South)
Highest League scorer during career:	Grenville Morris, 199, 1898-1913
Most League appearances:	Bob McKinlay, 614, 1951-70

Transfers In: Jean Claude Darcheville (Rennes £700,000).
Tranfers Out: Kevin Campbell (Fenerbache undisclosed fee)

Nottingham Forest

Middlesbrough

Above: *Marco Branca.*
Ross Kinnaird/Allsport

Right: *Paul Gascoigne.*
Mark Thompson/Allsport

There's no doubting the anguish felt by the team and fans who watched Middlesbrough's fall from the Premiership 1996-97 in spite of a handful of top South American stars. On top of this, heartbreaking cup losses to Chelsea, the last to two extra-time strikes in the 1997-98 Coca-Cola Cup, would have destroyed a less resilient team. But Brian Robson's squad has taken on the pugnacious heroism shown by the manager every time he walked out onto a pitch as a player, and no-one will expect them to perform half-heartedly.

Founded in 1876, Middlesbrough joined the Second Division in 1899, and were promoted in their third season. They remained First Division regulars until the mid-1920s, finishing a creditable fourth in 1914, then suffered two brief spells back in the Second.

Between 1929 and the outbreak of hostilities, Middlesbrough established a reputation for attractive attacking football. Inspired first by the legendary George Camsell, whose 59-goal tally in the 1926-27 campaign still stands as a Second Division record, and then by local boy Wilf Mannion, capped 26 times for England, the side won many fans for their playing style, and in the final peace-time campaign they equalled their previous best by finishing fourth in the League.

The postwar period was to prove disappointing, and as Mannion's star faded so did the club's. By 1954, Middlesbrough had returned to the Second Division, and there they would stay, apart from a single season in the Third, until the mid-1970s. During this time, they were blessed with the gifts of the young Brian Clough, a prolific scorer who found the net 197 times in only 213 appearances, but even this was not enough to bring success to Ayresome Park. The arrival of Jack Charlton as manager heralded a return to the top flight in 1974, but the record since then has been patchy, with spells in all of the top three divisions and a flirtation with insolvency.

The 1995-96 season saw many changes for the Teesside club—a return to top-flight competition, the arrival of new manager Bryan Robson, and the move to the impressive new 30,000-capacity Riverside. Boro proved unable to retain their Premiership status, but bounced back in 1997-98, Paul Gascoigne the latest in a series of high-profile buys that had included fellow England international Paul Merson from Arsenal. With Sunderland having missed out on promotion and Newcastle in decline, the stage is set for Boro to become the region's soccer success story.

Season at a Glance

1997-98 Final Position:	2nd in Division One
Top League Goalscorers:	Beck: 14, Merson: 12, Branca: 9
Highest League win:	6-0 v Swindon (H), 11 March 1998
Worst League Defeat:	0-5 v QPR (A), 4 March 1998
Highest Attendance:	30,228 v Oxford United, 3 May 1998
Lowest Attendance:	29,414 v Charlton Athletic, 9 August 1997

Middlesbrough

Managers

John Robson	1899-1905
Alex Mackie	1905-06
Andy Aitken	1906-09
Andy Walker	1910-11
Tom McIntosh	1911-19
James Howie	1920-23
Herbert Bamlett	1923-27
Peter McWilliam	1927-34
Wilf Gillow	1934-44
David Jack	1944-52
Walter Rowley	1952-54
Bob Dennison	1954-63
Raich Carter	1963-66
Stan Anderson	1966-72
Jack Charlton	1973-77
John Neal	1977-81
Bobby Murdoch	1981-82
Malcolm Allison	1982-84
Willie Maddren	1984-86
Bruce Rioch	1986-90
Colin Todd	1990-91
Lennie Lawrence	1991-94
Bryan Robson	1994-

Above: *Manager Brian Robson.*
Ben Radford/Allsport

Right: *Paul Merson.*
Stu Forster/Allsport

Honours

Division One Champions:	1994-95
Runners-up:	1997-98
Division Two Champions:	1926-27, 1928-29, 1973-74
Runners-up:	1901-02, 1991-92
Division Three Runners-up:	1966-67, 1986-87
FA Cup Runners-up:	1997
Football League Cup Runners-up:	1997, 1998
Amateur Cup Winners:	1895, 1898
Anglo-Scottish Cup Winners:	1976

Transfers In: Gary Pallister (Man Utd £2.5m), Dean Gordon (Crystal Palace £900,000)
Tranfers Out: Nigel Pearson (retired)

172

Club Details

Year formed:	1876
Ground:	Cellnet Riverside Stadium, Middlesbrough, Cleveland TS3 6RS
Nickname:	Boro
Club Colours:	Red and white
Manager:	Bryan Robson
Record attendance:	Riverside Stadium: 29,469 v Manchester City, 9 December 1995, Premier League; Ayresome Park: 53,596 v Newcastle United, 27 December 1949, Division One
Record League victory:	9-0 v Brighton & Hove Albion, 23 August 1958, Division Two – Scorers: Clough 5, Harris 2 (2 pens), Peacock 2
Record Cup victory:	9-3 v Goole Town, 9 January 1915, FA Cup First Round – Scorers: Carr 3, Elliott 3, Tinsley 3
Record defeat:	0-9 v Blackburn Rovers, 6 November 1954, Division Two
Highest League scorer in a season:	George Camsell, 59, 1926-27, Division Two
Highest League scorer during career:	George Camsell, 326, 1925-39
Most League appearances:	Tim Williamson, 563, 1902-23

173

Middlesbrough

Charlton

Charlton Athletic's departure from the Valley, their traditional home in south-east London, in 1985 seemed to signal the beginning of the end for a club that, since missing the League Championship by just four points in 1937 and winning the FA Cup ten years later, had struggled to make a mark on the London football scene. Spells as tenants with firstly Crystal Palace and then West Ham led to a triumphant return to the Valley in 1992, supporters having fought local elections to ensure their voice was heard.

Under the guidance of manager Alan Curbishley (initially sharing the job with Steve Gritt), the Valiants strove to regain a top-flight place last enjoyed for a five-year spell under the shrewd management of Lennie Lawrence from 1986 and bring five-figure crowds back to the Valley. And in 1998 the promised land was attained, thanks to a dramatic penalty shootout win at Wembley in the play-offs against Sunderland.

Lawrence's most illustrious predecessor was Jimmy Seed, who reigned from 1933 to 1956 and presided over their halcyon days which included another FA Cup Final appearance, in 1946 when they lost to Derby County. His first season had seen a rise from Third (South) to First Divisions, thanks to the goalscoring of Ralph Allen and the shot-stopping of Sam Bartram, who was unlucky not to win international recognition.

The club has produced many promising players over the years including full-back Scott Minto, sold to Chelsea, England midfielder Robert Lee (Newcastle) and Lee Bowyer (Leeds). By hanging on to star defender Richard Rufus and splashing out on Clive Mendonca, the club record buy whose goals took them up, the Valiants showed their determination to stay in the top flight—although to do so will take more than just courage.

Above: *Steve Jones.*
Ben Radford/Allsport

Right: *Mark Kinsella.*
Stu Forster/Allsport

Season at a Glance

1997-98 Final Position:	4th in Division One
Top League Goalscorers:	Mendonca: 26, Robinson: 8, Bright: 7, S Jones: 7
Highest League win:	5-0 v West Brom (H), 3 March 1998
Worst League Defeat:	2-5 v Nott'm Forest (A), 22 November 1997
Highest Attendance:	15,815 v Nott'm Forest, 28 March 1998
Lowest Attendance:	9,868 v Sheffield United, 9 December 1997

Charlton

Managers

Walter Raynor	1920-25
Alex McFarlane	1925-28
Albert Lindon	1928
Alex McFarlane	1928-32
Albert Lindon	1932-33
Jimmy Seed	1933-56
Jimmy Trotter	1956-61
Frank Hill	1961-65
Bob Stokoe	1965-67
Eddie Firmani	1967-70
Theo Foley	1970-74
Andy Nelson	1974-80
Mike Bailey	1980-81
Alan Mullery	1981-82
Ken Craggs	1982
Lennie Lawrence	1982-91
Alan Curbishley & Steve Gritt	1991-95
Alan Curbishley	1995-

Above: *Manager Alan Curbishley.*
Tom Shaw/Allsport

Right: *Clive Mendonca.*
Stu Forster/Allsport

Club Details

Year formed:	1905
Ground:	The Valley, Floyd Road, Charlton, London SE7 8BL
Nickname:	The Addicks
Club Colours:	Red and white
Manager:	Alan Curbishley
Record attendance:	75,031 v Aston Villa, 12 February 1938, FA Cup Fifth Round
Record League victory:	8-1 v Middlesbrough, 12 September 1953, Division One – Scorers: Firmani 3, Hurst 2, O'Linn 2, Leary
Record Cup victory:	7-0 v Burton Albion, 7 January 1956, FA Cup Third Round – Scorers: Leary 3, Kiernan 2, Hurst, Gauld
Record defeat:	1-11 v Aston Villa, 14 November 1959, Division Two
Highest League scorer in a season:	Ralph Allen, 32, 1934-35, Division Three (South)
Highest League scorer during career:	Stuart Leary, 153, 1953-62
Most League appearances:	Sam Bartram, 583, 1934-56

Honours

Division One Runners-up:	1936-37
Division Two Runners-up:	1935-36, 1985-86
Division Three (South) Champions:	1928-29, 1934-35
FA Cup Winners:	1947
Runners-up:	1946
Full Members Cup Runners-up:	1987

Transfers In: Neil Redfern (Barnsley £1m), Chris Powell (Derby £850,000), Emeka Ifejiagwa (£20,000 Lagos) Simon Royce (Southend free) Andy Hunt (West Brom free)
Tranfers Out: Phil Chapple (Peterboro free)

Charlton

Chelsea's Mark Hughes
shows all his aggression
against Bolton. Allsport

Bolton Wanderers

Above: *Scott Sellars*
Mark Thompson/Allsport**.**

What a way to go! The champions of Division 1 went straight back down after only one season of Premiership football after tying with Everton on 40 points. The relegation issue was decided on goal difference in the end—and many would say the Trotters were the better of the two teams. Over the season, however, Everton had proved five goals better, and Colin Todd must have rued his falling out with former England star Peter Beardsley that took away a proven goal maker.

It had started well enough—a 1-0 win away win at Southampton, and a come-back from two down to draw at Coventry saw four points and three goals for Nathan Blake. September saw four draws and a loss to in-form Arsenal and October brought a victory against high-flying Chelsea, thanks to a goal from new signing Dean Holdsworth.

It would be the long nights of winter that put paid to the Bolton season: following the creditable home victory against Newcastle at the beginning of December, until the victory over Sheffield Wednesday on 14 March, there would be only five points from a possible 36, in spite of Blake's continued sharpness in front of goal.

Todd's team fought bravely: wins against Blackburn, Bolton, Aston Villa and Crystal Palace in the run-in gave them a last-game chance, but against Chelsea team spirit wasn't enough.

Bolton Wanderers were founder members of the Football League but success has not often come easily. Three 1920s FA Cup wins, a loss in the 'Matthews' Final against Blackpool in 1953 and another FA Cup win in 1958 were the glory days. But by the late 1980s they were in Division 4. In the 1990s manager Bruce Rioch proved impressive in his team-building on limited resources, and an FA Cup run in 1993-94 that saw off Everton, Arsenal and Aston Villa was followed by a Division One promotion season.

The loss of young Liverpool-born wide man Jason McAteer to his home-town team, followed by the defection of Rioch to Arsenal proved a double blow the Trotters fought in vain to survive, and after experimenting unsuccessfully with a management pairing of ex-Derby boss Roy McFarland and Colin Todd, Rioch's assistant manager was given the field to himself. Though relegated in 1996, the Trotters bounced straight back up with 100 goals and nearly as many points thanks to the twin international strikeforce of John McGinlay (Scotland) and Nathan Blake (Wales). Unfortunately, as is so often the case, Bolton lost McGinlay and Blake's heroics were insufficient to save a battling team in 1997-98. There's no doubt, however, that Bolton will be knocking on the door again in 1998-99.

Season at a Glance

1997-98 Final Position:	18th in the Premiership
Top League Goalscorers:	Blake: 14, Thompson: 10, Holdsworth: 3
Highest League win:	5-2 v Crystal Palace (H), 4 May 1998
Worst League Defeat:	5-0 v Sheffield Wed (A), 8 November 1997
Highest Attendance:	25,000 v Manchester Utd, 20 September 1997
Lowest Attendance:	23,703 v Wimbledon, 29 November 1997

97/98 Results

August

9	Southampton	A	W	0-1	Blake (43)
23	Coventry City	A	D	2-2	Blake (69, 76)
27	Barnsley	A	L	2-1	Beardsley (31)

September

1	Everton	H	D	0-0	
13	Arsenal	A	L	4-1	Thompson (13)
20	Manchester United	H	D	0-0	
23	Tottenham Hotspur	H	D	1-1	Thompson (pen 20)
27	Crystal Palace	A	D	2-2	Warhurst (9),Gordon (19)

October

4	Aston Villa	H	L	0-1	
18	West Ham United	A	L	3-0	
26	Chelsea	H	W	1-0	Holdsworth (72)

November

1	Liverpool	H	D	1-1	Blake (84)
8	Sheffield Wednesday	A	L	0-5	
22	Leicester City	A	D	0-0	
29	Wimbledon	H	W	1-0	Blake (89)

December

1	Newcastle United	H	W	1-0	Blake (22)
6	Blackburn Rovers	A	L	3-1	Frandsen (84)
14	Derby County	H	D	3-3	Thompson (pen 50), Blake (73), Pollock (77)
20	Leeds United	A	L	2-0	
26	Barnsley	H	D	1-1	Bergsson (38)
28	Everton	A	L	3-2	Bergsson (42), Sellars (43)

January

10	Southampton	H	D	0-0	
17	Newcastle United	A	L	2-1	Blake (72)
31	Coventry City	H	L	5-1	Sellars (21)

February

7	Manchester United	A	D	1-1	Taylor (60)
21	West Ham United	H	D	1-1	Blake (86)

March

1	Tottenham Hotspur	A	L	1-0	
7	Liverpool	A	L	2-1	Thompson (7)
14	Sheffield Wednesday	H	W	3-2	Frandsen (31), Blake (53), Thompson (pen 69)

Bolton Wanderers

| 28 | Leicester City | H | W | 2-0 | Thompson (52, 89) |
| 31 | Arsenal | H | L | 0-1 | |

April

4	Wimbledon	A	D	0-0	
11	Blackburn Rovers	H	W	2-1	Holdsworth (20), Taylor (67)
13	Derby County	A	L	4-0	
18	Leeds United	H	L	2-3	Thompson (56), Fish (89)
25	Aston Villa	A	W	1-3	Cox (18), Taylor (41), Blake (84)

May

| 4 | Crystal Palace | H | W | 5-2 | Blake (7), Fish (20), Philips (30) Thompson (70), Holdsworth (79) |
| 10 | Chelsea | A | L | 2-0 | |

Above: *John McGinlay.*
Shaun Botterill/Allsport

Below: *Manager Colin Todd.* Clive Brunskill/ Allsport

Right: *Nathan Blake* Graham Chadwick/ Allsport

Honours

Division One Champions:	1996-97
Division Two Champions:	1908-09, 1977-78
Runners-up:	1899-1900, 1904-05, 1910-11, 1934-35, 1992-93
Division Three Champions:	1972-73
FA Cup Winners:	1923, 1926, 1929, 1958
Runners-up:	1894, 1904, 1953
Football League Cup Runners-up:	1995
Freight Rover Trophy Runners-up:	1986
Sherpa Van Trophy Winners:	1989

Club Details

Year formed: 1874
Ground: Burnden Park, Bolton BL3 2QR
Nickname: The Trotters
Club colours: White and navy blue
Manager: Colin Todd

Record attendance: 69,912 v Manchester City, 18 February 1933, FA Cup Fifth Round
Record League victory: 8-0 v Barnsley, 6 October 1934, Division Two—Scorers: Westwood 4, Taylor 2, Milsom, opposition own goal
Record Cup victory: 13-0 v Sheffield United, 1 February 1890, FA Cup Second Round—Scorers: Cassidy 5, Weir 4, Brogan 3, Robinson
Record defeat: 1-9 v Preston North End, 10 December 1887, FA Cup Second Round

Highest League scorer in a season: Joe Smith, 38, 1920-21, Division One
Highest League scorer during career: Nat Lofthouse, 255, 1946-61
Most League appearances: Eddie Hopkinson, 519, 1956-70

Bolton Wanderers

Barnsley

Above: *Neil Redfearn*
Stu Forster/Allsport

The scenes of triumph in May 1997 when Barnsley reached the top level for the first time in the club's 110-year history were not to be repeated on Premiership pitches in 1997-98. But the Tykes have got nothing to be ashamed of: they went down with their heads held high and memories of victories against such luminaries as Liverpool and Aston Villa.

The problem was the defence—82 goals against and 23 losses sunk Danny Wilson's brave team. Early season drubbings by Chelsea (6-0), Arsenal (5-0) and Manchester United (7-0) showed how difficult the season would be.

The outstanding player for Barnsley was Neil Redfearn, who will stay in the Premiership with recently promoted Charlton in 1998-99. He scored 14 goals and was always an inspiration. The highlight of the season was the FA Cup run which saw Barnsley close to an FA Cup semi-final. Unfortunately for their Yorkshire supporters, they lost to eventual finalists Newcastle. On the way they had beaten Bolton, Tottenham and, most memorably, Manchester United after a replay.

Formed in 1887 as Barnsley St Peter's, Barnsley have been members of the Football League since 1898 when they were elected to the enlarged Division Two. Since then, they've mainly inhabited the lower divisions, though since 1981, when they achieved promotion under the management of ex-Leeds and England defender Norman Hunter, they've stood one rung off the top division.

Hunter was one of three ex-Elland Road bosses in a decade, following Allan Clarke and preceding Bobby Collins, yet it was the management team of Viv Anderson and Danny Wilson, transplanted from Sheffield Wednesday in 1993, that gave the club grounds for optimism.

There can be few Tyke supporters still alive that can remember the glory days when the team won through to the FA Cup Final twice in three years, both occasions going to replays. Despite losing to Newcastle at Goodison in 1910, they emerged victorious by a single extra-time goal against West Bromwich at Bramall Lane two years later. A marathon Cup run included 14 matches in all, their spirit typified by a defender who took a boot off to have his foot attended to, yet sprinted back on without it to clear an attack (this would not be allowed today!).

Season at a Glance

1997-98 Final Position:	19th in the Premiership
Top League Goalscorers:	Redfearn: 14, Ward: 10, Fjortoft: 6
Highest League win:	2-0 v Coventry (H), 20 October 1997
Worst League Defeat:	7-0 v Manchester Utd (A), 27 October 1997
Highest Attendance:	18,692 v Tottenham, 18 April 1998
Lowest Attendance:	17,463 v Coventry, 20 October 1997

97/98 Results

August

9	West Ham United	H	L	1-2	Redfearn (9)
12	Crystal Palace	A	W	0-1	Redfearn (56)
26	Chelsea	H	L	0-6	
27	Bolton Wanderers	H	W	2-1	Tinkler (12), Hristov (47)
30	Derby County	A	L	1-0	

September

13	Aston Villa	H	L	0-3	
20	Everton	A	L	4-2	Redfearn (32), Barnard (78)
23	Wimbledon	A	L	1-4	Tinkler (41)
27	Leicester City	H	L	0-2	

October

4	Arsenal	A	L	5-0	
20	Coventry City	H	W	2-0	Ward (11), Redfearn (pen 66)
27	Manchester United	A	L	7-0	

November

1	Blackburn Rovers	H	D	1-1	Bosancic (79)
8	Southampton	A	L	4-1	Bosancic (pen 37)
22	Liverpool	A	W	0-1	Ward (35)
29	Leeds United	H	L	2-3	Liddell (8), Ward (28)

December

8	Sheffield Wednesday	A	L	2-1	Redfearn (29)
13	Newcastle United	H	D	2-2	Redfearn (9), Hendrie (75)
20	Tottenham Hotspur	A	L	3-0	
26	Bolton Wanderers	A	D	1-1	Hristov (20)
28	Derby County	H	W	1-0	Ward (67)

January

10	West Ham United	A	L	6-0	
17	Crystal Palace	H	W	1-0	Ward (26)
31	Chelsea	A	L	2-0	

February

7	Everton	H	D	2-2	Fjortoft (24), Barnard (63)
21	Coventry City	A	L	1-0	
28	Wimbledon	H	W	2-1	Fjortoft (25), (63)

March

11	Aston Villa	A	W	1-0	Ward (17)
14	Southampton	H	W	4-3	Ward (17), Jones (32), Fjortoft (42), Redfearn (pen 57),
28	Liverpool	H	L	2-3	Redfearn (37), (pen 85)
31	Blackburn Rovers	A	L	2-1	Hristov (67)

Barnsley

April

4	Leeds United	A	L	2-1	Hristov (44)
11	Sheffield Wednesday	H	W	2-1	Ward (65), Fjortoft (72)
13	Newcastle United	A	L	1-2	Fjortoft (50)
18	Tottenham Hotspur	H	D	1-1	Redfearn(19)
25	Arsenal	A	L	2-0	

May

| 2 | Leicester City | A | L | 1-0 | |
| 10 | Manchester United | A | L | 0-2 | |

Above: *David Watson*
Ben Radford/Allsport

Right: *New Player-manager John Hendrie in action* MikeHewitt/Allsport

Far Right: *Former Manager Danny Wilson* /Allsport

Honours

Division One Runners-up:	1996-97
Division Three (North) Champions:	1933-34, 1938-39, 1954-55
Runners-up:	1953-54
Division Three Runners-up:	1980-81
Division Four Runners-up:	1967-68
FA Cup Winners:	1912
Runners-up:	1910

Club Details

Year formed:	1887
Ground:	Oakwell Ground, Grove Street, Barnsley, South Yorkshire S71 1ET
Nickname:	The Tykes, Reds or Colliers
Club colours:	Red and white
Manager:	John Hendrie
Record attendance:	40,255 v Stoke City, 15 February 1936, FA Cup Fifth Round
Record League victory:	9-0 v Loughborough Town, 28 January 1899, Division Two – Scorers: Davis 4, Jones 2, Hepworth, Lees, McCullough; 9-0 v Accrington Stanley, 3 February 1934, Division Three (North) – Scorers: Blight 4, Spence 2, Smith, Andrews, Ashton
Record Cup victory:	6-0 v Blackpool, 20 January 1910, FA Cup First Round replay – Scorers: Lillycrop 2, Tufnell 2, Boyle, Gadsby; 6-0 v Peterborough Utd, 15 September 1981, Football League Cup First Round, second leg – Scorers: Glavin 2, Parker 2, Aylott, Barrowclough
Record defeat:	0-9 v Notts County, 19 November 1927, Division Two
Highest League scorer in a season:	Cecil McCormack, 33, 1950-51, Division Two
Highest League scorer during career:	Ernest Hine, 123, 1921-26 and 1934-38
Most League appearances:	Barry Murphy, 514, 1962-78

Barnsley

Crystal Palace

Above: *Atillo Lombardo*
Ben Radford/Allsport

Poor old Palace. It all looked so wonderful on 23 August 1997. Six points were in the bag, and new signings Atillo Lombardo (£1.6 million from Italian Serie A) had scored twice and Paul Warhurst (£1.5 million from Blackburn) once. True there had been a rather dispiriting home loss to fellow-Premiership newcomers Barnsley, but surely a Selhurst Park victory wouldn't be too far away?!

By the time that home victory arrived on 18 April 1998 against Derby County, courtesy three final quarter goals, Palace were all but relegated. Injuries and lack of performance at home combined with off-the-field problems had sunk what appeared on paper to be a team of great potential, improved in November by the signing of Italian striker Padovano for £1.7 million.

When Chairman Ron Noades moved Steve Coppell upstairs to become Director of Coaching and made Lombardo manager, he was ending his days in charge of Palace with a flourish. He would leave in May, replaced by Mark Goldberg, at the end of three months' much-publicised negotiations, during which Terry Venables name was on everyone's lips as the man Goldberg wanted in the manager's job. With this going on in the background, it is hardly surprising that Palace struggled on the field of play.

Terry Venables had been associated with Palace before. Up to his arrival as player-coach to Malcolm Allison in 1976, Crystal Palace's history had been a chequered one. Ex-Swindon boss Bert Head had attained First Division status from 1969-73 with a mixture of bargain buys, veterans from the Scottish League, the occasional foreigner and home-grown keeper John Jackson. All reached their sell-by date simultaneously and the arrival of Allison saw a second successive demotion. After rebounding to Division Two in 1977, Venables went for youth to form the Team of the 1980s around the youth Cup-winning team of 1977 and 1978 which he'd coached: only defenders Kenny Sansom, Jim Cannon and Paul Hinshelwood survived. The side secured the title in 1979

The next man to exert a Venables-like influence was Steve Coppell, also in his first management role. The ex-Manchester United and England winger took Palace up in 1989 with a team that harnessed the exciting strike talents of Ian Wright and Mark Bright. The same side took his former team United to within an ace of the FA Cup in 1990, but let a 3-2 lead slip and lost 1-0 in the replay. Bright and Wright were sold, the team subsided in 1993 and Coppell resigned only to rejoin in 1997 and win the play-off Final against Sheffield United to gain promotion to the Premiership.

Season at a Glance

1997-98 Final Position: 20th in the Premiership
Top League Goalscorers: Dyer: 8, Shipperly: 7, Bent: 5, Lombardo: 5
Highest League win: 3-1 v Sheffield Wed (A), 25 October 1997
Worst League Defeat: 6-2 v Chelsea (H), 3 May 1998
Highest Attendance: 26,186 v Chelsea, 11 March 1998
Lowest Attendance: 14,410 v Wimbledon, 9 February 1998

97/98 Results

August

9	Everton	A	W	1-2	Lombardo (36), Dyer (pen 77)
12	Barnsley	H	L	0-1	
23	Leeds United	A	W	0-2	Warhurst (22), Lombardo (51)
27	Southampton	A	L	1-0	
30	Blackburn Rovers	H	L	1-2	Dyer (51)

September

13	Chelsea	H	L	0-3	
20	Wimbledon	A	W	0-1	Lombardo (80)
24	Coventry City	A	D	1-1	Fullarton (9)
27	Bolton Wanderers	H	D	2-2	Warhurst (9), Gordon (19)

October

4	Manchester United	A	L	2-0	
18	Arsenal	H	D	0-0	
25	Sheffield Wednesday	A	W	1-3	Hreidarsson (27), Rodger (52), Shipperley (60)

November

3	West Ham United	A	D	2-2	Shipperley (19, 45)

(Game abandoned after 65 minutes due to floodlight failure; fixture re-arranged)

8	Aston Villa	H	D	1-1	Shipperley (42)
24	Tottenham Hotspur	A	W	0-1	Shipperley (67)
29	Newcastle United	H	L	2-1	Shipperley (57

December

3	West Ham United	A	L	4-1	Shipperley (42)
6	Leicester City	A	D	1-1	Padovano (43),
13	Liverpool	H	L	0-3	
20	Derby County	A	D	0-0	
28	Southampton	H	D	1-1	Shipperley (62)
28	Blackburn Rovers	A	D	2-2	Dyer (12), Warhurst (48)

January

10	Everton	H	L	1-3	Dyer (pen 17)
17	Barnsley	A	L	0-1	
31	Leeds United	H	L	0-2	

February

9	Wimbledon	H	L	0-3	
21	Arsenal	A	L	1-0	
28	Coventry City	H	L	0-3	

March

11	Chelsea	A	L	6-2	Hreidarsson (7), Bent (87)

Crystal Palace

14	Aston Villa	A	L	3-1	Jansen (62)
18	Newcastle United	A	W	1-2	Lombardo (14), Jansen (23)
28	Tottenham Hotspur	H	L	1-3	Shipperley (82)

April

11	Leicester City	H	L	0-3	
13	Liverpool	A	L	2-1	Bent (72)
18	Derby County	H	W	3-1	Jansen (73), Curcic (80), Bent (90)
27	Manchester United	H	L	0-3	

May

2	Bolton Wanderers	A	L	5-2	Gordon (8), Bent (16)
5	West Ham Utd	H	D	3-3	Bent (44), Rodger (48), Lombardo (63)
10	Sheffield Wednesday	H	W	1-0	Morrison (90)

Above: *Bruce Dye.* /Allsport

Right: *Paul Warhurst and Dean Blackwell.* Dan Smith/Allsport

Far Right: *Jon Newsome and Neil Shipperley.* Allsport

Next Page: *David Beckham.* Allsport

Honours

Division One Champions:	1993-94
Division Two Champions:	1978-79
Runners-up:	1968-69
Division Three (South) Champions:	1920-21
Runners-up:	1928-29, 1930-31, 1938-39
Division Three Runners-up:	1963-64
Division Four Runners-up:	1960-61
FA Cup Runners-up:	1990
Zenith Data System Cup Winners:	1991

Club Details

Year formed:	1905
Ground:	Selhurst Park, London SE25 6PU
Nickname:	The Eagles
Club colours:	Red and blue
Manager:	Attilio Lombardo and Tomas Brolin
Record attendance:	51,482 v Burnley, 11 May 1979, Division Two
Record League victory:	9-0 v Barrow, 10 October 1959, Division Four – Scorers: Summersby 4 (1 pen), Byrne 2, Colfar 2, Gavin
Record Cup victory:	8-0 v Southend United, 25 September 1990, Rumbelows League Cup Second Round first leg – Scorers: Bright 3, Wright 3, Thompson, Hodges
Record defeat:	0-9 v Burnley, 10 February 1909, FA Cup Second Round replay; 0-9 v Liverpool, 12 September 1990, Division One
Highest League scorer in a season:	Peter Simpson, 46, 1930-31, Division Three (South)
Highest League scorer during career:	Peter Simpson, 153, 1930-36
Most League appearances:	Jim Cannon, 571, 1973-88

191

PREMIER LEAGUE FOOTBALL